APR - - 2014

B PARSIPUR, S.
Parsipur, Shahrn+½sh.
Kissing the sword :a prison memoir /

P9-CJF-200

WITHDRAWN

KISSING the SWORD

A PRISON MEMOIR

Shahrnush Parsipur

TRANSLATED BY SARA KHALILI
FOREWORD BY ROBERT COOVER

THE FEMINIST PRESS
AT THE CITY UNIVERSITY OF NEW YORK
NEW YORK CITY

Alameda Free Library
1550 Oak Street

Published in 2013 by the Feminist Press
at the City University of New York
The Graduate Center
365 Fifth Avenue, Suite 5406
New York, NY 10016

feministpress.org

Translation copyright © 2013 by Sara Khalili

All rights reserved.

Originally published in 1996 in Sweden as *Prison Memoir*
by Baran Publishing.

No part of this book may be reproduced, used, or stored in any information
retrieval system or transmitted in any form or by any means, electronic, mechanical,
photocopying, recording, or otherwise, without prior written permission from
the Feminist Press at the City University of New York, except in the case of brief
quotations embodied in critical articles and reviews.

ART WORKS.
arts.gov
*This book is supported in part by an award from the
National Endowment for the Arts.*

State of the Arts
NYSCA
*This book was made possible thanks to a grant from
New York State Council on the Arts with the support of
Governor Andrew Cuomo and the New York State Legislature.*

First printing March 2013

Cover design by Faith Hutchinson
Text design by Drew Stevens

Library of Congress Cataloging-in-Publication Data
Parsipur, Shahrnush.
[Khatirat-i zindan. English]
Kissing the sword / Shahrnush Parsipur ; translated from the Persian by Sara Khalili.
pages cm
Originally published as: Khatirat-i zindan. Sp?nga, Sweden : Baran, 1996.
ISBN 978-1-55861-816-9 (pbk.)
1. Parsipur, Shahrnush. 2. Authors, Iranian—20th century—Biography.
3. Political prisoners—Iran—Biography. I. Title.
PK6561.P247Z46 2013
891'.558303—dc23
[B]

2012043902

Foreword

SAVAGERY IS A DEFINING CONDITION OF THE animal kingdom, but only humans, blessed with reason, can invent death camps, inquisitions, the subtle instrumentation of torture, mass executions. We continually amaze ourselves with viciousness, the cause of which is less often bloodlust or brutality than it is mere expediency. Certain persons threaten our authority and well-being, and the easiest and most effective means to get them out of the way is to exterminate them. For protesting the execution of two leftist poets, Shahrnush Parsipur was imprisoned the first time and sentenced to two months in solitary confinement by the shah of Iran, a cruel and ruthless man who used his CIA-created secret police, SAVAK, to do his dirty work; but when the citizens grew restless, he resisted US "iron fist" advice, proving to them his essential weakness, and in 1979 his regime fell to the powers who control this narrative. The ayatollah and his revolutionary guards had more backbone. Within a short time, they had rounded up not only the royalists, but also their revolution's former allies, the secular leftists and the Islamist-Marxist Mujahedin, and the slaughter began, the success of which is evidenced by the regime's continuance (and continued political executions) to this day.

The surviving witnesses of such mass killings are often silenced by fear or oppression, or worse, a broken spirit. Not so the gifted and resilient author of this harrowing memoir, imprisoned three times by the Islamic Republic of Iran, the first time for four and a half punishing years, eventually driven into exile by the threat of further arrests and harassment, her health by then seriously damaged, her writings banned, her pockets empty, but ever keeping faith with her chosen vocation as a writer and unbending witness to her times. *Kissing the Sword* is a deeply moving, closely observed classic of its form, and would be viewed as such, no matter who its author, but when they imprisoned Shahrnush Parsipur, they picked on one of the world's greatest and most determined living authors. Indeed, the first draft of *Touba and the Meaning of Night*, an epic masterpiece in the same league with *One Hundred Years of Solitude* and *Midnight's Children*, was scribbled into notebooks, as readers will discover here, during the terrible ordeal of her long imprisonment. She is the author of nearly a dozen other works of fiction, written before and after that time, most famously perhaps *Women Without Men*, made into an award-winning film by the video installation artist Shirin Neshat.

Kissing the Sword is a searing depiction, with very little self-pity or moralizing, of a living nightmare. It quietly celebrates, amid unspeakable horrors, such virtues as decency, integrity, thoughtfulness, concern for others—these being other inventions of the human animal. And honesty: nothing goes unsaid. The narrative often shocks, sometimes touches, almost always dismays, its most appalling discovery perhaps being that, upon release from prison's cruel theater, the nightmare does not end. It is only less structured.

—Robert Coover

Los Angeles, December 21, 1995

I T IS THE FIRST DAY OF WINTER. THE SUN RISES.

I bow down in prayer. I believe that all existence is conscious. I believe that every speck of dust somehow—dust like—is conscious. I believe that you cannot find two hydrogen atoms that are identical. I believe that hydrogen atoms, too, are somehow conscious. And so, I pray:

> *God, I praise you in all your manifestations. This is you*
> *burning yourself in one scene so as to come forth in others.*
> *This is you who at times wish not to be, so that all at once*
> *you can overwhelmingly be. This is you who wished that I*
> *witness your death and rebirth in a sea of blood. Give me*
> *the power to write that which I have seen in prison.*

Work is always a savior and my work is to write. I have lived through difficult years and in the past two, I have been suffering from a severe nervous disorder. A vague pain creeps up my vertebrae and into my brain. I tell myself, Time is short, if you don't write now you may never have another chance. I think of the millions of books gathering dust in huge libraries. Amid all these, what value could my work really have? Yet, this is the only thing I know how to do. I tell myself, Write! Don't worry that it may not be read. It is the age of the computer and every day people in the advanced world grow more distant from the old world, every day a new discovery is tested and professors in their great rush cannot write their books and instead hand them to their students as notes. But, don't worry, write. Perhaps someone will read it.

One day in the communal cellblock at Ghezel-Hessar Prison, at the time of evening prayers, which coincided with the television news hour, we learned that an American space shuttle with seven crewmembers onboard had exploded. They showed footage of the explosion. As always, when important news was being broadcast, there was a great commotion. The prisoners all ran toward the television and the details of the news were lost in the noise. This always upset me. Television was our only window to the world, and even I who didn't have a natural affinity for it, had come to depend on it. On another occasion, when I was in Disciplinary Unit 8, the news story being broadcast was about the leader of one of the leftist groups whose members were being persecuted by the government. Obviously, the prisoners who were supporters of that party were quite interested, but again, much of the information was lost in the clamor of people jostling for a place in front of the television. That time, I suddenly screamed, "Shut up!" A strange silence fell across the unit and we managed to hear the tail end of the story. People who know the etiquette of dancing always know when to be still, when to move, and when to be silent. But unfortunately, dancing is considered shameful in present-day Iran.

When the American space shuttle exploded, the prisoners all looked upset. I was puzzled. Since the start of the Islamic Revolution in Iran, "Death to America" had been the constant slogan of the Islamic Republic; at Friday prayers the crowd would start by chanting "Death to America, death to Israel." It always surprised me that, at least in the early days, they didn't chant "Death to the Soviet Union." After all, the Soviet Union had a communist government and the Hezbollah, which was in power, was deeply opposed to communism. I concluded that being in close proximity to this giant was reason enough not to shout such slogans. But the fear and respect of our neighbor to the north did not seem to extend to the prison officials. They had ordered the Soviet and American flags to be painted on the ground outside the prison's main entrance so that one would have to walk over them to enter the compound.

It had gotten dark outside and the guards had closed the doors to the courtyard. I desperately needed to get some fresh air and stood next to the door to the courtyard, wishing I could be out there. A young girl of perhaps seventeen walked up to me and in a somber tone asked if I had heard the news about the space shuttle. I nodded and said, "Don't you all constantly claim that you're opposed to America? Then why has news of the shuttle exploding upset you so much?" She looked at me wide-eyed and said, "But this is science. It is humankind's knowledge. It belongs to everyone."

So there was America, which we identified with the slogan "Death to America," and alongside it there was science, which belonged to humankind and united all societies. I spent the entire next day thinking about this. I thought about religions spreading across the world, crossing boundaries and cultures; science had proved to have a similar universal appeal.

I was deep in these thoughts when I caught sight of a girl who always wore a green dress with floral patterns. She walked constantly, for days at a time, without breaking stride. It was the beginning of her mental illness.

I remembered the moment of my arrest and all that had happened since. I had thought that after my release from prison, I would write my memoir. It was the day after the shuttle exploded that the thought occurred to me, but for various reasons writing it was delayed for years and it became more or less a dead issue. Now, in Los Angeles, in Beverly Hills, in a completely American environment, I have taken up my pen and I am searching for a beginning.

I have been to prison four times. I have never been accused of a crime, except for the third time, and that charge was based on falsified evidence, as the court later agreed. During my years in prison, I never took notes. In general, throughout my life, I have never jotted down notes. Therefore, I may make mistakes in providing specific dates. I have also forgotten the names of many of the prisoners. But, to the extent that memory serves, I promise to be just and accurate in recreating events.

Tehran, August 13, 1981

1 I WAS HOME. IT WAS EVENING. I HAD JUST taken a shower and was resting when the doorbell rang. I answered the intercom and the person identified himself as being from the Islamic Revolutionary Court. I walked out onto the balcony and called down to him and his two companions in a loud voice so that the neighbors, or at least the doorman, would become aware of my situation. They came up to the apartment, gave me a summons, and searched the rooms. I got dressed. Knowing that I had committed no wrong, I naively thought that I would be detained and questioned for no more than forty-eight hours. I was confused and not thinking clearly. On leaving the apartment, I took only enough money to pay for a taxi ride home and nothing more. I took no personal effects, not even a toothbrush, but I locked the doors to all the rooms, something we never did at home, and took the keys with me.

They took me to Evin Prison, the infamous prison built during the reign of the shah and operated by his feared secret police, the SAVAK. At the main entrance, they blindfolded me but I could tell that even at that late hour—it was around midnight—there were many people coming and going. They led me into a corridor and had me stand in a corner. From beneath my blindfold, I could see there were other people standing there. One person was trembling violently and moaning. After some time, they led me into a room, sat me down on a chair, and removed my blindfold. An olive-skinned man with a bushy beard was sitting in front of me. He was in his late twenties. My attention was drawn to the large diamond ring he was wearing. I had never seen a man wear a diamond ring, except for a wealthy and flamboyant industrialist I met during the shah's era, and he popped into my mind at that moment.

The interrogator wrote several questions on a sheet of paper and I answered them in writing. My first name, family name, and then my opinion of various political groups. I think the first one was about the monarchy, to which I replied, "By the will of the people, that government fell in 1978." He then asked about the "cursed" Banisadr, the first president of the Islamic Republic of Iran who had been impeached and had fled to France just a few weeks earlier. I wrote, "I imagine Mr. Banisadr has made certain mistakes." My interrogator then asked about the "hypocrites' organization"—a term Ayatollah Khomeini and the Hezbollah used to describe the Islamist-Marxist People's Mujahedin of Iran, his one-time allies who were now being suppressed—and I replied, "I don't know the Mujahedin that well and I don't have a particular opinion of them."

In all my answers, I tried to be respectful of all people and groups. The interrogator finally shouted, "What is this? Everyone is a mister to you?" I answered, "Yes, and the day you fall off your horse, you too will be a mister to me."

I had been arrested once before, in 1976 during the reign of the Shah, and spent fifty-four days in solitary confinement for having resigned from my job as a producer at the National Iranian Radio and Television in protest of the arrest and execution of several artists and writers. I had moved to France after my release to escape the suffocating environment that had engulfed the country. But in France financial pressures and loneliness weighed heavily on me. By 1980, with Iran in the throes of revolution and turmoil, I found myself incapable of moving on with my life. A tragedy was unfolding in my homeland. I could see the specter of bloodshed. I could see an ailing state—seven thousand years old and forty million people strong—in the convulsions of death, throngs of people being killed with each tremor. As a writer I felt directionless and weak, and I could not define my role as an individual. I didn't have the courage to throw myself into the arms of the world, and my lack of identity in a foreign land made me even less daring. Although I was a published writer and my books had been well-received in Iran, I thought that if I wanted to gain recognition for my work, I had to return and live in my country.

In the summer of 1980, I sent my son to Iran to live with his father and attend school there. I started shipping my collection of books related to my Chinese studies at the Sorbonne—I was translating Laozi and the Taoist masters—to Iran. By September, I was ready to return but war broke out between Iran and Iraq and travel to the country became restricted. I spent my evenings next to the radio, following the news. The day they announced the reopening of Tehran's airport, I went to Orly

Airport, where as fate would have it, a passenger had not shown up and I took his seat.

Six months of apathy followed. The country was in a revolutionary crisis, the economy had collapsed, and rival Islamist and leftist political factions were vying for power. I had moved into my mother's apartment. While I was looking for work, I went to the tedious and chaotic meetings of the Writers Association. Soon, however, I realized that because I was neither a revolutionary nor a member of a political group, I had no role there. Still, the meetings were my only social outlet.

Walking along the city streets, I would often stare at the faces of the young political activists selling newspapers and I was certain that most of them would be killed. My fear compelled me to write a letter to Massoud Rajavi, the leader of the Mujahedin. In it I tried to explain that, now that the Ayatollah had turned on his group, there was no way for their organization to come to power and that a mass killing was inevitable. I wrote that it would be prudent to order the youth to return to their homes and to save their lives before it was too late. I also wrote about the futility of armed conflict. I read the letter to two friends, both of whom said that it was useless and would serve no purpose. I threw the letter on my desk and decided not to send it, but I didn't tear it up; I had worked hard on it and it was well-written.

In May, my brother Shahriar and a few of his friends started a video club and they put me in charge of it. Being employed meant that I would soon be able to bring my son, who was still with his father, to live with me, and to feel that I was slowly settling down in Iran.

I spent my days at the video club calling well-to-do people in the hopes of bringing in more members. Meanwhile, I was translating Mircea Eliade's three-volume *A History of Religious Ideas* from French to Persian. The work on Eliade was influenced by my thinking about the *Enûma Eliš*, the Babylonian myth of creation, which describes the god Marduk's elevation above all others, and the epic of Gilgamesh, with its tale of Tammuz's murder at the hands of his lover, the goddess Ishtar. These are among the earliest mythologies of the world, and are considered humanity's earliest written texts. At that stage of the revolution in Iran, I could not stop thinking about the meaning and significance of these myths.

On the morning of June 28, 1981, I was getting ready to leave for the video club. Despite Hezbollah's propaganda, women were still not obligated to cover themselves, and I remained stubbornly hijabless. My mother turned on the radio. They were broadcasting a religious mourning ceremony. We wondered who had died.

On the way to the office, I saw that the streets were emptier than usual, emptier than they were even on holidays. The front door of the building where the club was located was locked and I didn't have a key. I returned home and called my brother who told me there had been a massive explosion at the headquarters of the ruling Islamic Republic Party (IRP) and many had been killed. I told my mother what had happened. We took my three year old niece, who had spent the night with us, and drove to my brother's house. There, I learned that the large number of people killed included Ayatollah Mohammad Beheshti, the secretary general of the IRP and head of the Islamic Republic's judicial system. I was shocked by news of his death. He was a very powerful man and had played an important role in the revolution.

All that I was afraid of was becoming reality. For several days, newspapers had been publishing photographs of young political activists, men and women, who had been executed. The bloody times were moving along.

While I was discussing all this with a few friends in the living room, my mother and brother were having a different conversation in the kitchen. My brother told her that he and his friends had been collecting an archive of political periodicals published by leftist and communist groups. He said their reasoning was that once the Islamic government solidified its control over the country, all opposition groups would be suppressed and their publications would be confiscated; his archive would be valuable for future studies. I believe that was the extent of my brother's political activities. But by then, he had a large collection of anti-government publications in his house.

A few nights before the bombing of the IRP headquarters, the warden of Evin Prison and the chief judge of Tehran's Islamic Revolutionary Court had appeared on television and announced that all opposition political publications were banned, and anyone caught with them would be sentenced to the most severe punishment. Now my brother, whispering in the kitchen with my mother, was trying to get rid of the pamphlets. He didn't have a car, so he asked my mother to put them in the trunk of her car and to either throw them away in ruins outside of town or hide them in the basement of her apartment building. My mother agreed.

A few hours later, my mother and I said our goodbyes and drove home. The streets were still empty. On Fereshteh Street, we saw barricades in front of a mosque. Ambulances were driving by carrying motorcycles inside their open doors instead of patients. I didn't understand the reason for this. It was perhaps to ferry the strike forces to a new location.

My mother forgot all about the suitcase in the trunk of her car and a few days later, on July 3, she drove to Evin, a neighborhood in northern Tehran, to visit my younger sister who was pregnant. Evin Prison is there, and it was common for the revolutionary guards to stop and search the cars driving nearby. My mother casually waited as they inspected her car. Of course they discovered the suitcase. They asked her what the periodicals were and she told them they were Mujahedin publications. Although there were many opposition political groups, my mother was only familiar with the Mujahedin. And when they asked her who they belonged to, she said they belonged to her. The guards told her that they would have to take her to Evin Prison for her to explain her case. My mother innocently asked whether she could first stop by my sister's house to drop off the things she had brought for her. Delighted to learn where she was heading, the guards agreed.

According to the doorman at our apartment building, that morning as I walked out through the garage to take out the garbage, the revolutionary guards entered the building and went up to our apartment. Unaware, I went to the office. I had just sat down at my desk when my brother called, terrified. He told me that our sister had called to say our mother had been arrested. My mind went blank, then I told my brother to go to our apartment because there were many political newspapers and magazines there, too. I used to buy one or two every week, each belonging to a different faction, and after reading them, I would toss them in a corner in the kitchen.

Meanwhile, my younger brother, who lived with us, returned from a trip to Mashad in northeastern Iran, one of the holiest cities in the Shia Muslim world, and came straight to the video club to see me. I told him what had happened and asked him to go to the apartment as well and keep an eye out for the revolutionary guards. Afraid that the guards would show up at the office to question me, I gave him my address book and asked him to throw it in a trashcan on the street.

It was not until five years later that I learned what happened that day. My brothers both arrived at my mother's apartment at about the same time. The revolutionary guards were there searching the apartment. My older brother told them that the publications they had found in my mother's car belonged to him. Regardless, the guards turned the apartment inside out and arrested both of my brothers. Among the items they took were my records and cassette tapes. They ripped up some of my books, and from my French and Chinese collections they took the first volumes of each series and left the rest behind. They also found the letter I had written to Massoud Rajavi.

I sat waiting in the office, expecting one of my brothers to call. I was concerned, but I didn't really think the incident would take a serious turn. At about three in the afternoon, one of the video club partners arrived, and after discussing the situation, we concluded that I should return home and not come to work for a few days.

Seeing the apartment ransacked terrified me. The doorman suggested that I run away. Despite my fear, I told him I didn't think it would be necessary, that we hadn't done anything that would require me to flee. I still thought they would hold my mother and brothers briefly and the whole incident would be over. I watered the plants and started tidying up. I didn't dare throw all the newspapers and magazines in the garbage and decided instead to burn them in the toilet. The fire caused the toilet to crack, so I stopped.

That night I sat and watched television. Again the head of Evin Prison and the chief judge appeared on the screen, reading the names of people who had been executed that day.

I stayed home for two days. I thought of everyone I could contact for help and in the end I decided to try to see Azam Taleghani, who was a member of parliament and the daughter of the highly respected Ayatollah Taleghani. I thought she would not only sympathize with my plight, but would have the power to help me. This truly showed how little insight I had. My mother and brothers had been dragged away and were completely cut off from communication. What could this woman do? Nevertheless, I wrote a note to her, explaining that my family members were in danger and that they were not at all politically active, and I went to the parliament building and gave it to one of the guards to deliver to her. After some time, a man approached me and with a smile asked how I was and inquired about Shahriar. It turned out he was the representative from the city of Khormashahr and one of my brother's childhood schoolmates. The guard had somehow given my note to him and he had recognized my last name. Relieved, I explained the situation to him and he promised to do whatever he could. He even said he would ask Akbar Hashemi Rafsanjani, then chairman of the parliament, for a personal note.

A few days later, I again went to the parliament. My brother's friend had kept his word and had a handwritten note from Rafsanjani asking the warden of Evin Prison to attend to the case of the Parsipurs. I gave the note to my sister-in-law who took it to Evin Prison and handed it to one of the guards at the main entrance. I didn't keep a copy of it.

By then, my mother and brothers had been in custody for well over a week and we had had no news of them. I resumed my work at the video club and kept in regular contact with my brother's friend, but I soon got the feeling that he was trying to distance himself from me. On August 13, I too was arrested.

The interrogator continued with his endless questions. Then he asked about the letter I had written to Rajavi. "The letter was never sent to him," I explained, "and, in fact, it touches on issues that are not in disagreement with the Islamic Republic. As an Iranian, I have tried to explain to the leadership of this organization that an armed movement is a mistake." He asked about a trip I had made to Kurdistan a few months earlier to interview the dissenting leader of the Kurdish people for an article that was published in a literary magazine edited by an influential Iranian poet, Ahmad Shamlou. I answered that the tone of the interview clearly demonstrated that I was not in favor of Kurdistan seceding. He asked about the pamphlets they had found in my mother's car and I, not knowing what my mother and brothers had said, claimed they belonged to me.

The interrogation finally ended and they took me to a solitary cell. The unit's prison guard was a thuggish woman who dressed in masculine clothes and had a bad temper. The next night they again interrogated me and this time they put me in a cell right above the prison bakery's oven; it was unbearably hot. I was there for three days and on the fourth night I was transferred to the common prison block.

Evin Prison, Infirmary Section

2 THEY REMOVED MY BLINDFOLD IN THE MAIN office of the women's section. I had come to prison wearing corduroy pants, a button-down shirt, and a small headscarf. My clothes were by now filthy. One of the guards called for a girl named Minu, who managed the room where I was to be imprisoned, and handed me over to her. Together we entered the unit. Throughout the shah's era, this section that now housed women political prisoners had served as the infirmary, which is why it was comparatively spacious. The windows were large and the rooms felt homey. There were pieces of carpeting everywhere and to keep them clean, all the prisoners went barefoot.

In the summer of 1980, the shah's last prime minister, Shapour Bakhtiar, had attempted to overthrow the newly formed government of the Islamic Republic. Known as the Nojeh plot, the plan involved mostly high-ranking officers of the armed forces, all of whom, like Bakhtiar, were monarchists. They were discovered and more than one hundred people were arrested, several women among them. At that time, the government claimed that it had no political prisoners. To keep up this pretense, those arrested in connection with the attempted coup were held in the infirmary and now we were all put there, sharing it with the women who had been part of the Nojeh plot. Farrokhru Parsa, Iran's first female cabinet minister under the shah, had been led to the firing squad from this unit. Many of the Nojeh prisoners had befriended the guards in order to make their lot easier, and were put in charge of the daily chores in the section.

In the winter and spring of 1981, many more people were arrested, mostly from the People's Mujahedin of Iran and other leftist groups, and brought to Evin. The Mujahedin and the majority of the leftists were Marxists, but the Mujahedin were strictly religious while the others were secular. The three main groups of inmates—the monarchists, the Mujahedin, and the secular leftists—had divided the prison rooms among themselves, with each group assigned its own area where they lived according to the traditions of their own beliefs. Remnants of the spirit that dominated the early days of the revolution still lingered.

When my mother was first brought in, she had been delivered to the Mujahedins' room because she had linked the publications found in her car to that group. But within a few days, it had become apparent to everyone that she should be handed over to the monarchists; she didn't cover her hair, and her manner and disposition were more in tune with that of the monarchists and the nationalists. I was taken to the same room because she was there.

When I walked into the room, I saw some fifteen women gathered around my mother; they were sitting there, cheerfully chatting. My mother seemed happy, which astonished me. During all the weeks when I had no news of her, I had been beside myself with worry. Now she looked like she was on holiday.

After a while, I too was in good spirits. The prisoners had learned to make the passing of time more tolerable by telling stories, sharing memories, and reading books. But among them was a girl named Golshan, who was profoundly sad. I was told that a week earlier, her father had been executed for being a monarchist. I tried to be kind to her and soon we became friends. I learned that in the room across the hall there were others with similar circumstances. One of them was a woman whose sister had been executed along with Golshan's father.

On my second day, I went for a stroll around the unit. The rooms were packed with people, but one could still breathe. It was the first time I had the opportunity to observe the different political groups. During the shah's era, I had not been drawn to the Mujahedin or their politics, and I was against their insistence on mandatory hijab. After the revolution, I continued to disapprove of them. Their ideology wasn't clear to me, but I knew enough to know that as fanatical Islamist Marxists they wanted a theocratic government, and I believed in the separation of religion and state. But their organization seemed to be growing exponentially.

According to one apocryphal story, in February 1979, at the start of the revolution, Fidel Castro sent a telegram to Massoud Rajavi and Moussa Khiabani, the two leaders of the Mujahedin. They decided to reply in their own individual names. But a poet who supported the Mujahedin suggested that they send the telegram in the name of the organization. Rajavi said that was silly because they had only sixteen members. Now, in August 1981, some one hundred women and girls accused of being Mujaheds were being held in the infirmary unit alone. There were surely more of them in the other sections, and just as many men, if not more, in the men's areas.

The Mujahedin were strangely keen on addressing women who had children as "mother." In order for these mothers not to be confused with one another, and for their real identity not to be revealed, they gave themselves distinct names: Blue Mother, Mother Sadigheh. Among them was a woman they called Haaj Khanoom, an honorific for one who has gone on a pilgrimage to Mecca. She was an authoritative woman who was highly respected and at times even feared. I remember she had her own private clothesline in the prison courtyard and no one dared walk past it.

A large number of the Mujahedin were perpetually fasting. They would eat together at sunrise and then fast the rest of the day. During my early days in prison, this irritated me. The Prophet of Islam had dedicated only one month per year to fasting and I couldn't understand the meaning of this constant denial. And then a girl who belonged to a leftist group in Kurdistan enlightened me: Fasting helped them sustain their revolutionary spirit and increased their physical tolerance for hardship.

The older Mujahed women were for the most part deeply religious, often superstitious, and fairly close minded. But the younger ones tended to be more open and educated, and they easily mingled with the other groups while making every effort to show respect to their elders.

It took twenty-four hours for me to figure out my place. I was neither a monarchist, nor a leftist. To me it was irrelevant what title the country's leadership bore, whether monarchy or republic. What mattered most was to be fair and unbiased, and that was how I tried to behave.

I decided to start a French class. A large number of leftists and a handful of Mujahedin and monarchists joined the class. The monarchists were not too happy to be taught alongside leftists, but I explained to them that before all else, we were equal members of Iranian society and that I had respect for everyone. As far as I was concerned, one of the core problems of our society was intolerance and the desire of all groups and parties to completely eradicate the others. In prison, I was struggling to swim against this current. The end result was that the monarchists avoided discussing important issues in my presence for fear I would share information with the leftists, while the leftists accepted me only as a conditional friend.

I learned that the leftist groups kept all their money in a collective box and the person in charge of finances would shop at the prison commissary for all of them. No one spent their own money on themselves. They all handed their funds over to the person in charge. They also shared all their clothes, since most of them had been arrested on the street and had no belongings with them. Even their undergarments were communal. The seventy-member leftists' room had only two towels. Fortunately, they didn't have any diseases, although later, fungal infections became a prisonwide problem.

The leftists held meetings to discuss all their purchases. Buying fruits that didn't have essential vitamins was prohibited. Nor would they buy confections or luxury food items. And they always set aside a special fund for the needs of pregnant and ailing women. Once they invited me to their room to celebrate a prisoner's birthday and they distributed four and a half raisins to each of us. A few sticks of chewing gum were also carefully measured and dispensed. I think each stick was divided into eight pieces that were so small mine got lost in my mouth.

I found the communists' principles interesting, if comical. I compared their ways with the system in the monarchists' room, where everyone kept their own money and each person shopped according to her own means. As a result, at breakfast one person would have three jars of jam in front of her while another would have none. Many with meager budgets felt obliged to buy certain items so as to appear equal to the others, but some were in a bad way, with no money at all. I had arrived in prison with only my hurriedly grabbed cab fare and until friends or family brought me money, I had difficulty buying necessities from the commissary, let alone luxuries. Occasionally wealthier people among the monarchists would take the needy under their wing. But these acts of charity often cultivated subservience.

Every day residents of a different room were responsible for carrying out the various tasks in the unit, including cleaning.

Among the leftists, other than the pregnant and the sick, everyone worked. Among the Mujahedin, the older women were exempt and the girls would divide the chores among themselves. In the monarchists' room, it was the elderly who were excused. But Minu had decided to singlehandedly prove to all the other groups that the system in our room was the best and therefore created an incredible amount of work for herself. She even offered financial help to those among our roommates who had no money. I once cautioned her that she was taking on far too much responsibility and that perhaps it would be best to set up a shared savings box. Of course, not in the same manner as the leftists, I assured her, but so that each person would deposit some money, which could be used to support needy prisoners. She vehemently disagreed with me and continued to bear the financial burden all by herself. She also took over the cleaning duties of the elderly women in the room, rather than parcel them out. Amid the chaos of blood and horror that was soon to begin, she was turning into a paragon of hard work and labor.

A week after I started my French class, word came from the prison's administration office that it must stop. So, to keep myself busy, I started making prayer beads together with several other prisoners. We used bread dough to make the beads and painted them with watercolors.

By then, the prisoners were regularly being taken from the unit to be interrogated. They would often wear very large slippers instead of their shoes, because most often their feet would be whipped. Without the slippers, they would have to walk back barefoot on lacerated and swollen feet. The back and forth shuttling of these prisoners to the prosecutor's office was gradually instilling an atmosphere of terror in the unit. But because there were so many inmates, with new ones being brought in every day, we did not fully grasp how many prisoners were being tortured.

On August 31, I took a survey. I wrote down the results but the guards forced me to tear it up. Today, I write relying on memories that never fade. I measured the area of the unit, including the hallways, toilets, and showers and divided it by 165—the total number of prisoners in the unit at the time. Each prisoner had slightly more than five square feet of space. In reality, it was impossible to move around the rooms at night; everyone slept on the floor, pressed together. The average age of the prisoners was nineteen and a half, with the youngest prisoners no more than fourteen years old. More than eighty percent were high school students; some ten to fifteen percent were university students; and the rest were teachers, nurses, housewives, and office workers. Based on this, it seemed we were facing a high school student rebellion. Even the director of the women's prison was a nineteen year old girl. At that crucial point in history, some of the most critical affairs of the state were to a great extent determined by teenagers and young people in their twenties.

I was eager to take a survey of the occupation of everyone's father, but in the beginning most of the prisoners would not share more than silence with me. In the months that followed, as greater trust developed among us, I was able to gather some information regarding the women's backgrounds. In general, the left-leaning prisoners came from urban middle-class families. The Mujahedin, on the other hand, belonged mostly to migrant rural populations. Either they had come from their village to the city on their own, or their fathers had brought their families. Many of the Mujahedin had relatives who were supporters of Ayatollah Khomeini and even held government jobs and positions.

On September 7, 1981, they took my mother and me to stand trial. We sat in a courtroom all day, blindfolded. We were tried separately. I remember I was acting stiff and formal. I was angry. From the way the judge was questioning me, it was clear that he knew there were no serious infractions in my record. Regardless, in accordance with Iranian tradition—based on a landlord-peasant social structure—as the accused, I was expected to sit there humbly with bent back, addressing the judge as "your honor," and referring to myself as "your servant."

The courtroom was comprised only of a judge and a secretary. There was no defense attorney, and as far as I can remember, I was not asked any questions directly related to our case. There may have been one inquiry about the publications. Instead, the judge wanted to discuss issues such as my belief in God, man's will, and the like. He even raised a question about incest between a father and daughter. I didn't understand the reason for this question, but I said that I knew of a few such cases and that the problem was deeply rooted in history. I mentioned the story of Lot in the Old Testament, who had sexual relations with his daughters. That night, one of the prisoners told me that several months earlier a retired prostitute had been held in the unit and questioned about various forms of sexual relations during her trial. The prosecutor's behavior had been so offensive that the poor woman had felt greater shame and degradation than she had ever experienced in a lifetime of prostitution.

When the time came for our bread-and-cheese lunch break during the trial, they had me sit in the hallway next to a girl who was lying on the floor. Earlier that day, she had sat near me and asked one of the guards to bring her jacket which she had left behind in a court room; she was cold. When the guard brought the jacket, he quietly whispered, "Farideh, Farideh, what have you done to yourself?" The girl did not answer. And then, at lunch, she was there lying next to me. I peeked at her from beneath my blindfold and she laughed at me. Then she asked, "How are things in the unit?" Without knowing which unit she was referring to, I said, "All is well." She said, "My name is Farideh Shamshiri. Say hello to everyone for me."

That night I told my roommates about her and they all became quite excited. I learned that Farideh had been brought to the unit in the winter, and to keep herself busy she painted, using supplies provided by the unit administrator, who had noticed her talent. Every morning and evening she went to the unit office to pick up and return the art supplies and soon these frequent visits became a subject of discussion among her fellow inmates, and rumor spread that Farideh was cooperating with prison officials. Given the seriousness of the accusation, to prove her loyalty to the leftist prisoners, Farideh stopped painting and participated more and more in antigovernment slogan chanting, which the authorities were trying to prevent. The end result was that one day the guards raided the unit, beat everyone severely, and transferred Farideh to solitary confinement. They also installed a speaker in front of one of the windows and started broadcasting their own slogans and readings from the Quran at earsplitting levels. According to those who knew, even in solitary confinement, Farideh continued to chant slogans and to write them in pencil on the walls.

The day after I saw her, reports of Farideh Shamshiri's execution appeared in the newspapers. The news shocked everyone. Those in the unit who had pushed her toward her death by spreading rumors about her were devastated.

But an hour had barely passed after we learned of Farideh's death when the sound of laughter again echoed everywhere. The prisoners were still at an age when joyfulness is one's natural state of being. Even though the unit was becoming more crowded, with three or four people added every day, the young girls rarely complained. Many of them knew each other and were happy to see one another again—even if it was in prison. Or they instantly made friends and tried to get news of the world outside.

Often I would watch as the prisoners who were called in for questioning left the unit. I could easily tell whose case was more serious by the demeanor of her friends—they would follow her to the door with solemn faces and anxious expressions. Being young and inexperienced, many of them had divulged all their group's secrets to each other, and now they were worried about what would be confessed to under torture.

Around the time of my trial, a few people arrived in the unit whom others called *tavvāb*—"repentant." They were members of different political groups who had confessed to all manner of actions and deeds and had promised to cooperate with the authorities. In exchange, they were granted certain liberties and worked as guards in the units where they were being held. The tavvābs were generally cruel and ruthless and were feared and despised by the prisoners. Their arrival ignited new tension and anxiety in the unit.

A few weeks passed, and I was still waiting for the outcome of my mother's and my trials. The population in the unit continued to increase and it became impossible to walk in the courtyard. There was less food. The morning piece of cheese was getting smaller and there were no visitors to bring money so that people could buy food from the commissary to make up for the shortage. Occupants of certain rooms claimed they were given less to eat than the others and it soon became apparent they were not lying. The Mujahedin were under greater pressure than the other groups. Day by day, their numbers increased, their food decreased, and a sense of constant fear and apprehension came to reign over them.

The number of prisoners being physically tortured was

increasing. Many were black and blue all over. I remember Shahin from those days, a woman with dark olive skin, who was affiliated with a leftist group. One day they took her to the public prosecutor's office and gave her a severe beating. When she returned to the unit, I asked her to show me her bruises. She laughed and said that because of her dark skin her bruises didn't show. The next night, I saw Shahin in the bathroom, cheerfully chatting with a friend. She had been interrogated again that day, and it seemed she had escaped danger. But two days later, she looked worried and upset. She had been summoned to the public prosecutor's office again. The following afternoon, we found her name among those who had been executed. I asked one of her friends what Shahin had been accused of. Her friend said she had been caught driving a car with a printing machine in its trunk. On the last day of her life, Shahin had told her friend that she thought they were going to execute her because the interrogator had touched her breasts; to her this meant that she was going to be put to death.

In truth, I never heard prisoners talk about sexual abuse. But it was rumored that on their final night, young girls sentenced to death were wed to the guards so that they wouldn't be buried as virgins. It was said that if a girl was buried while still a virgin, she would lure a man to follow her to the grave. My only proof that this might have been happening were Shahin's last words. I did know a couple of other prisoners who had gotten close to having sexual relations with the guards, but in one instance it was a prisoner's strategy to stop her torture, and in another,

deeply affectionate feelings had developed between an interrogator and a prisoner.

By the end of September, the number of prisoners who could
no longer walk had soared. Their feet were swollen to the size of
oranges. The worst part was that they had great difficulty using
the Chinese-style squat toilets. As a result, a group of prisoners
built a sort of western-style toilet using a large, empty cheese
can. They covered the rim with a strip of thick foam ripped
from a mattress and tied it in place with a piece of yarn; two or
three people would lift a prisoner and sit her down on the toilet.

3 I THINK IT WAS ONE OF THE LAST NIGHTS of September. I had been in prison for more than a month. The doors to the courtyard had just been closed when they announced, "All prisoners must exit to the courtyard." A crowd of more than two hundred and fifty stood crammed together in the small yard. After a while, they announced, "You may return to the unit, but you are not to enter the television room."

We went back into the building, but without access to the large television room, we were still crammed together. The crowd swarmed everywhere, barely able to breathe. One of my friends, a Kurdish girl, asked whether I had seen her friend Razieh. I had not. She said they had brought Razieh into the television room and I should go see her there. I told her the tavvābs were most certainly with Razieh and they would report me if I walked into the room. The Kurdish girl replied, "Since you're a writer, you should see her so you'll know what a human being can be made to look like."

I went to the room and, pretending that I wanted to watch television, I opened the door. Razieh Al-Taher was lying on a bed in the middle of the room and three young tavvābs were sitting around her. They looked terrified. Razieh's leg was bandaged from the sole of her foot up to her thigh. From the ooz-ing blood and puss, the bandage had turned the color of rust. Razieh turned and looked at me. She raised her hand. It was as if she wanted to say something, and she remained like that for a while. She had bruises under her eyes. I asked the tavvābs why her eyes were bruised. One of them said she had a high fever. I walked out to avoid creating problems for myself.

Razieh Al-Taher is one of the few names I can still remem-ber from those days. It was said that her father was a mullah who was killed in the demonstrations that led up to the rev-olution. She had joined the Mujahedin after the revolution. Her crime was that she had made a duplicate key to the front door of her school and at night she would use the photocopy machine to make copies of the organization's manifesto. Her friends said it was one of her relatives who had turned her in to the authorities.

Half an hour later, they again moved us to the courtyard so that they could transfer Razieh to some other place. People who were taken in for questioning the next day said they had seen her in a wheelchair, delirious, hallucinating, and unable to control her bowel movements.

The following night, past one o'clock in the morning, I thought I should take advantage of the late hour and go to the bathroom so I could avoid the long lines in the morning. The prisoners were all lying down pressed against each other. But it seemed everyone was awake. We had been hearing ear-split-ting noises from the courtyard since about eleven o'clock. One of the tavvābs had explained that they were building visitors' rooms and that the noise was steel beams being dropped to the ground.

There was no line at the bathroom door. Instead, several girls had gathered around the radiator and were taking turns climbing on top of it so that they could look out from a window set high in the wall. When I walked out of the bathroom, one of the women, Iran, climbed down from the radiator. She was shaking. Although we were not friends, she took me by the arm and whispered that the bodies of executed prisoners were lying on one side of the courtyard. Just then, we heard a loud noise again, and Iran started to shake even more. "What is that noise?" I asked her. "Heavy machine gun fire," she answered. Uneasy, I walked back to my room.

Earlier that day, I had seen two girls leave the unit. They were very beautiful and looked alike. They were wearing shoes and to avoid dirtying the pieces of carpeting on the floor, they crawled toward the door on their knees. I spoke to them and learned that both were seventeen and although they looked like twins, they were aunt and niece. I had not seen them return.

When I reached my room, Farideh, who managed the room across the hall, was standing in the doorway. She explained that when they carried out mass executions, they first used heavy machine guns and the sounds we'd been hearing were the shower of bullets. After each barrage of bullets, a single shot was delivered to the head of every prisoner to make sure they were dead. Farideh said the women in our unit were lying awake, counting the single shots. So far, they had heard more than ninety.

I stood in silence, listening. Again, the image of the young aunt and niece flashed in my mind. I went back to my room and told all this to Golshan and the others. We, too, started to count the shots. At around two in the morning, two girls from the leftists' room who had been summoned to the public prosecutor's office returned to the unit. Everyone followed them to their room, touching them. They had all believed the girls were among those executed that night and thought they were seeing ghosts.

The night of the heavy machine gun fire passed bitterly. We counted more than two hundred fifty single shots. Later we learned that several prisoners from each unit had been taken to the prosecutor's office earlier that night and had been hastily tried, each trial lasting no more than a few minutes. Then they were divided into two lines along the corridor—one to be put to death, the other to return to prison. One prisoner had been forced to sit for hours at the table where they had piled up the belongings of those sentenced to death. She sat there and stared at the toothbrushes, towels, and overcoats, and counted the single shots. They returned her to the unit the following morning, her face a mask of terror. One of the prison guards ran off in fright when she saw the look on her face.

The prisoners started a sullen day. A girl was brought to the unit who said her name was "Hulu," or "Peach." The Mujahedin had the habit of giving a false name when they were arrested and in prison they would go by the name of a fruit, a flower, or an animal. Hulu truly looked like her name. With tears in her eyes, she said she had died four times since her arrest. Twice the revolutionary guards had stormed the van she was being transported in and had pretended they were about to open fire on the prisoners. Another time she and several other prisoners had been lined up along a wall and the firing squad had shot blank shells at them. I can't remember the fourth incident. Hulu was fifteen, and it seemed as if something had died in her. I was consumed with barely suppressed rage. I was incapable of understanding why they were inflicting such horrors on the country's youth. At that moment, in the Islamic Republic's prison, I felt I had become a witness to and a partner in the bitter destiny of these children. But I still had a long road ahead of me before I would discover the darker aspects of the new, revolutionary Iran.

They brought us newspapers in the afternoon. I saw a list of some three hundred men and women who had been executed. Many relatives of prisoners in our unit were on the list, most of them leftists. I felt I should extend my condolences to them and I think it was from that day on that my circumstances grew more precarious, because to the authorities, if I was being kind to a leftist, I must be one of them. Also on the list was one of the two pretty girls I had seen leave the unit. The newspaper claimed she had been executed because she had committed adultery. I never tried to find out whether it was the aunt or the niece who was killed. I knew that in Islam they stoned adulteresses, but four unbiased witnesses had to have seen the act of adultery. I wondered in what situation they could have found this girl that would explain putting her in front of a firing squad. Again, I felt an excruciating sense of hatred. When I met the two girls, I remember thinking, I wish I had a daughter as beautiful as they are.

One night the guards announced an extraordinary situation and locked the doors to all the rooms. A prisoner suggested we sleep fully clothed. It was rumored that the Mujahedin were going to raid the prison. Crammed together in our room, it was difficult to breathe. Nothing particular happened, except that Minu was forced to singlehandedly wash the dinner plates of close to three hundred prisoners and returned to the unit soaking wet.

Another night soon after, the machine guns were again blasting until dawn and another group of prisoners lost loved ones. This time, the fifteen year old son of a woman in our unit was among those killed. She had four children and she lost three of them to the firing squads.

Every Friday evening the prison held a special prayer ceremony, the Komeil prayer, during which everyone was expected to weep and mourn. The ceremony was broadcast on the prison loudspeakers for several hours. I was raised in a Muslim family and although I don't abide by the tenets of Islam, I have never lost my respect for the religion. Now in prison, I was being exposed to religious rituals that bore no resemblance to what I was familiar with. The Komeil prayer, which had previously been performed by only the most traditional Muslims, was now expected of everyone. The loudspeakers, blaring into our unit, were nerve-racking.

One Friday night, a mullah dressed in an army jacket commonly worn by the revolutionary guards came to the unit and assembled us in the largest room. He had come to ask about the difficulties the prisoners were facing, he said. Normally, the prisoners didn't dare speak up, but by then they were so worn down that they complained about the noise of the heavy machine guns and the mass killings. The mullah denied it altogether and said, "It's the sound of a soccer ball hitting the rain gutters." And then, as is customary, he began to preach a sermon and suggested that the prisoners cry.

That day a vague understanding of the ritual of weeping during religious ceremonies began to take shape in my mind. The prisoners were all in such an emotional state that they needed to cry, and this man, who was one of the causes of their circumstances, had come there to encourage them to do so.

By the middle of November, the prison population had reached the point of explosion. More than three hundred fifty prisoners swarmed around the unit. At night some were forced to stand against the walls because there wasn't enough room to even sit, let alone lie down on the floor. The trials and executions continued and even these were becoming routine.

One day they announced the names of a great many prisoners and said they should prepare to be transferred to Ghezel-Hessar Prison. My name was among them. Golshan, the girl whose father had been executed as a monarchist, was also being sent there. My mother, who didn't want to be separated from me, went to the unit's administration office and managed to get her name added to the list.

I was tired and dispirited. I felt the weight of all the corpses on my shoulders. In truth, deep in my heart I was also somehow happy that I was in prison during that terrifying time. When you are free, you inevitably feel compelled to act, but in prison, you are powerless. If I had been free at that moment and had taken no action, I would have been deeply disappointed in myself. The breadth of the disaster unfolding was far greater than my capabilities, far greater than even the capabilities of the largest political groups.

Albert Camus wrote, "One must imagine Sisyphus happy," pushing his rock up a mountain only to have it roll back down again, because he has to be. And in prison, at a time of blood, filth, and stupidity, I was somewhat happy because I had to be. I had not wished the circumstances I found myself in, yet I did not try to alter them, and now the decision-making was left to the limited aptitude of the Hezbollah.

Ghezel-Hessar Prison, Unit 4

4 ONE MORNING, THOSE OF US WHO WERE being transferred to Ghezel-Hessar, some one hundred prisoners, were blindfolded and put on minibuses. We were all detainees who had stood trial, such as it was. Before our departure, the warden walked onto our minibus, turned to my mother, and said, "Do you know you've been sentenced to death?"

I was stunned. As the revolution seethed around us, my mother's involvement in politics had amounted to nothing more than listening to the news on the radio, if that could be considered political. And in a letter she once described mullahs as cats wearing Arab-style sandals, but this couldn't possibly result in a death sentence! In prison, my mother was always cheerful and kind to everyone. Like many others, she did not fully grasp the gravity of her situation. In reality, at the age of fifty-seven, prison was some sort of an adventure for her, although even she was beginning to lose her spirit.

The minibuses left Evin Prison's compound and our blindfolds were removed so that we would not attract attention while traveling along city streets. An hour later, we arrived at Ghezel-Hessar. Above the main entrance was a large sign that read, "Garbage Dump of History." We entered history's waste depository. Unlike Evin, which had a very complex configuration, Ghezel-Hessar had a simple structure that resembled a centipede. It had a very long main corridor with eight units that reached out from it like legs, with courtyards nestled in between them. We were in Section 3 of Unit 4. Our section was made up of eight subdivisions—four were communal and four had solitary confinement cells.

When we entered, they lined those of us from Evin on one side of the long corridor and had the prisoners being transferred from elsewhere stand on the opposite side. They, too, numbered close to one hundred. We were taken to the solitary confinement area, which, with the exception of a handful of prisoners, had been evacuated for us. There were twelve solitary confinement cells, one shower room with three stalls, and a restroom with three toilets. Each solitary cell measured approximately eight feet by five feet and contained a triple bunk bed with enough room between the bed and the wall for one person to pass.

They divided us among these "solitary" cells, fifteen to eighteen prisoners in each. Again, we were arranged leftists together, Mujahedin together, monarchists and the undecided together. My mother and I were put in a cell with a dozen others who, like us, were considered non-political prisoners. There was no mention of her death sentence.

With so many people stuffed into each cell, it was impossible to close the doors, but what did it matter? There was no place to escape to. From that day on, one of our main preoccupations was where to put our belongings.

That night they served *abgoosht* (lamb shank soup) for dinner. We were all surprised. There had been plenty of meat at lunch, too. We were told that during the last months of the shah's rule, the political prisoners at Ghezel-Hessar had gone on a hunger strike. Even prisoners who did not necessarily support Ayatollah Khomeini felt compelled to strike in support of the people's movement. The government of the shah, recognizing that its support outside the prison walls was in danger, decided to allot a daily quota of a half-pound of meat per day to each prisoner, expecting that word of its largess would be repeated by visitors. This arrangement lasted until about a month after I arrived at Ghezel-Hessar, and then prison food again became beggarly in quality and quantity.

After dinner, I went for a walk around the unit and saw a strange scene. A girl was stretched out on the floor next to the food mat, panting from having eaten too much. I asked the others what was going on and learned that for months before their transfer to this unit, these prisoners had been held in a residential building that used to house SAVAK employees during the shah's times. Eventually, the number of prisoners in the building's eight apartments had increased so much that they were as overcrowded as we had been in Evin. But their greatest misfortune was that because the building was located outside the main prison compound, it was often either forgotten or the last to receive an allotment of food. To make matters worse, the prisoners had no access to the commissary. With every person receiving little more than a spoonful of soup, they were always half-starved. Their circumstances would worsen when there was a pregnant woman among them. People who shared a meal with her would have to pretend to be full so that she would get a few mouthfuls of nourishment. One girl told me that she would often bury her head under her bedcovers and suck on the corner of her blanket. It took several days for the prisoners transferred from the SAVAK apartment building to be able to eat normally.

Within a few days of our arrival, an announcement came over the loudspeakers: Iran and Farzaneh, two monarchists who had come with us from Evin, should get ready to return there. At Evin, with the machine gun fire ricocheting off the walls so many nights, they had been certain they would be executed any day, and saw the move to Ghezel-Hessar as a good omen. They had immediately ingratiated themselves with the warden and had been put in charge of chores such as picking up the unit's shopping from the commissary. Now they both turned white. The next day, we read news of their execution in the newspaper. I was told that Iran was the person who kept the official seal of the Crown Prince during the monarchy. And supposedly Farzaneh had been involved in subversive plots with one of the colonels in the shah's army. But who knew if any of this was true? And in a prison populated mainly by Mujahedin and leftists, the death of two monarchists did not cause a ripple.

Among the prisoners who were already at Ghezel-Hessar when we arrived was a woman named Pari, who was accused of being a monarchist. In fact she didn't belong to any political group, but was an opium addict and a smuggler and had been arrested because monarchist fliers were discovered stuffed between the cartons of Winston cigarettes she was peddling.

She was first taken to Evin where she was confined to the infirmary to detoxify. One day, Mrs. Nourbakhsh, the warden, went to inspect the infirmary, and a girl in a locked cell, who belonged to a Marxist-Leninist group, begged to speak with her. Mrs. Nourbakhsh unlocked the door and the girl attacked her, wrapping her arms around Mrs. Nourbakhsh's neck and squeezing with all her might. Pari, weak as she was, struggled to her feet, made her way over to them, and managed to loosen the girl's arms from around Mrs. Nourbakhsh's neck. Now Pari was both a prisoner and a guard in our unit, responsible for locking and unlocking doors for the leftists. The warden, Haji Davoud, had banned them from leaving their cells, except for times when they needed to use the bathroom or the shower. Pari was a bully and harassed everyone for no reason. She would slam the padlocks against the steel bars and when the leftists needed to use the bathroom she would refuse to let them out of their cell. She wasn't mean or vicious by nature, she just thought this was how she was expected to behave.

It was said that Pari had been victimized as a child, which instilled a certain amount of sympathy for her among the others. And even though she drove everyone to despair, they tried to help her advance. Some two hundred people, most of them political activists, found themselves helping a single member of the masses. Meanwhile, she took the top bunk in her cell. Given that a crowd of seventeen had to live in that small space, she had quite regal accommodations.

One day Pari showed us many balls of yarn, which she said were from a sweater she had unwoven and asked us to knit gloves and socks for her. Ten of us agreed and we started knit-ting. In four days a pile of gloves and socks were knit for Pari. I wondered how she had really come to have all that yarn. Not long after, one of the tavvābs warned us not to take other peo-ple's clothes when they were out in the courtyard for recreation. The mystery was solved. For the first time I felt compelled to report someone, and I told the tavvāb about Pari's yarn, but I was certain they wouldn't be too harsh on her. The entire affair ended with a veiled warning from Haji Davoud.

Once, when I was in Pari's cell she suddenly screamed, "God! Reveal yourself to me!" Just then, a sparrow flew in through the window and sat on her lap. Behind the bars on the window there was a screen with a small tear in one corner. That was the first and the last time I ever saw just a moment's delay between a prayer and it being granted.

Our first major event at Ghezel-Hessar took place on the night of *Tasoua*—the eve of the death of Imam Hossein, a grandson of the Prophet Mohammad. For lunch before the holiday they served *zereshk-polo* (barberry rice with chicken), which was no less delicious than what the finest restaurants in town would offer. We were told that the SAVAK unit had offered to pay to feed all the prisoners in honor of the religious holiday. The SAVAK unit, sometimes called the "ungodly unit," was the special unit where prisoners directly affiliated with the shah were held. The group included a number of ministers, parliamentarians, high-ranking military officers, and wealthy individuals.

That night they gave us generous helpings of soup, cooked

with the livers of the chicken served at lunch. By then, all the hungry prisoners from the apartment building were well fed and no longer suffered from malnutrition. After six months of misery, torture, and executions, life seemed almost pleasant.

After dinner they announced that Tasoua's religious ceremonies would be held in the unit. The prisoners got ready to mourn, as is the custom on this holy day. Even the leftists put on headscarves or chadors and joined the ranks of the mourners. The atmosphere suddenly changed. The fact that leftists, Mujahedin, and monarchists had united made me strangely nervous. I went to my cell and picked up a notebook and a pencil, thinking I'd take advantage of the opportunity and jot down the verses that were going to be recited during the ceremony. Unfortunately, that notebook, along with all my other notebooks from prison, was later taken from me.

Golshan came to my cell and climbed up to the top bunk. She said she didn't have it in her to take part in the ceremony. I knew that up until her arrest she used to practice daily prayers, but now she had stopped praying altogether. She had been a third or fourth year student of mechanical engineering at a university in England, where she had participated in gatherings for students opposed to the revolution. As a young girl she had been active in the youth educational center that had been established by the shah and in general had no objection to a monarchical government. At the start of the Persian New Year, which coincides with the Easter holidays, she had come to Iran to marry her fiancé. But one day when she was visiting her father at his office, he was arrested along with other members of the group of monarchists he belonged to. Golshan was taken into custody also. She claimed that all she ever did for the group was to type one of their bulletins. Her father was executed, which affected her deeply. She was often obstinate and angry over insignificant issues. Like me, she never wore hijab.

Golshan told me about a dream she had while at Evin Prison. She had dreamed that she was held captive in the stomach of a centipede. A gigantic hand appeared and lifted the top off the centipede and took a number of people from inside the various cells in the creature's belly. Then the hand moved away and Golshan ran after it screaming, "Take me, too!" The hand put the people down on top of a hill and Golshan heard the voice of the hand saying, "I just wanted to bring them here." In prison, execution sites were called hills. Today, I regret that I didn't try to interpret the dream for her. I remember all I said was, "Golshan, be careful." By then, as was her habit, she had taken a few sedatives, which were widely available through the prison infirmary, and had buried her head under the blanket.

The mourning committee arrived—a guard and two tavvābs. All three were dressed in long black coats and large black headscarves, over which they were wearing black chadors. They stood at the head of the unit, facing everyone. Farzaneh, the guard, glared at me through my open cell door. Taken aback, I raised my notebook so that she could see it. She turned her gaze over to the first prisoner among the gathered group—a leftist who had put on a headscarf and was sitting on the floor. She pointed her finger at the girl and asked her, "What happened to Imam Hossein?" The girl thought for a moment and said, "He was killed."

Furious, Farzaneh shouted, "He was martyred!" The girl quickly corrected herself. "He was martyred," she repeated. Farzaneh then asked, "And Kalantary?" Everyone quickly realized that she was referring to one of the more than seventy-two people killed in the bombing of the IRP headquarters. The girl replied, "He was martyred." By then the prisoners knew they had to repeat that phrase in response to each name Farzaneh uttered. The list went on and with each name her voice grew louder and more impassioned and so did the responses from the prisoners. Suddenly, Farzaneh started beating her chest and she screamed, "And what became of my Beheshti? What? What?" And the crowd shouted as loud as they could for the secretary general of the Islamic Republic Party, whose death in the bombing just a few months earlier was the impetus for the round of terror that had brought us to prison: "He was martyred!"

Then the mourning began. The lights in our unit had been turned off and here and there candles were glowing through the dark. Prisoners who had lost relatives, and who under normal circumstances didn't dare mourn their loss, took advantage of the opportunity to grieve.

A Zoroastrian girl who was sitting next to my mother started beating her chest. Knowing that enduring such ceremonies was difficult for someone of a different faith, my mother turned to her and said, "My girl, it's all right. After all, Imam Hossein was your son-in-law." According to one story, Shahrbanou, the daughter of the last king of the Sassanid dynasty and a Zoroastrian, had been Imam Hossein's wife. The girl, still beating her chest, replied, "Fine, Imam Hossein is our son-in-law, but how are we related to Beheshti?"

Around two thirty in the morning, Farzaneh sat down and they placed a candle in front of her so that it would shine on her face. Then this former cabaret dancer, who turned out to be a talented actress as well, started to recite a eulogy for Imam Hossein and the martyrs of recent months. At five in the morning, the ceremony finally ended and the prisoners went to bed drained and exhausted.

The next day the guards distributed the supplies that families had brought for the prisoners. Without exception, every family had included a chador, which prison officials must have requested. Many families had also brought comfortable housedresses and some had included foods such as nuts and other snacks. There were a few blankets, too.

A girl showed up in our cell and said that the prisoners in the other cells had agreed to pool all the food they had received so that it could be divided equally among everyone. She asked whether we were willing to participate. We all agreed, but a few of my cellmates hid valuable foods such as pistachios and unashamedly accepted their share from the pooled supply. I confronted two of them and they both claimed that they needed the food more than the others did. Of course, everyone has the right to their own possessions, but what they received was far more than what they had contributed.

Soon after, because of other similar incidents, the prisoners lost trust in members of my cell and each time it was our turn to divide and distribute food, a few girls from other cells would come to oversee the process. Because of my cellmates' greed, the leftists, who had risen predominantly from among the working class, believed even more strongly that they could not trust more affluent people.

The other prisoners went so far in sharing that they even started eating out of the same plates and using the same utensils. Soon, a mouth infection spread throughout the unit. For a while, I avoided as best I could eating from the same plate as anyone else. I claimed that I had some sort of a problem with my gums and it was not right for me to risk infecting them. It took several months for everyone to agree to use their own plates and utensils again, after which they stopped suffering from infections.

THE DAY AFTER TASOUA, ALL THE LEFTIST prisoners joined the noon prayer. I thought their leaders had issued an order, but later I learned that their organizations had no such power at the time. Praying had been the prisoners' own decision, which, given our circumstances, was understandable. A few who trusted me admitted that one of them was reciting poems by Hafiz, another was simply moving her lips, and a third was counting from one to one hundred.

Still, I didn't pray. I strongly believed that I could never pray out of fear or praise God in a manner determined by the Hezbollah. I believed that if I did, I would lose my creativity to write. I believed, as I still do, that one of the secrets to being a writer is honesty with oneself. A writer might be a coward or an egotist, but if she is mired in dishonesty, the brilliance of her pen and the brightness of her mind will grow dark.

In the months that I had spent in prison, I had seen how quickly people changed from the tortures and executions and the constant emotional pressures. I had come to the conclusion that if I allowed myself to bend under pressure, then I would make it possible for the other prisoners to bend me even more. I didn't like the Islamic Republic any more than they did, but my belief in democracy made me want to preserve myself as I was and to make it clear to the others that I was not one of them. And so, with great trepidation and with the knowledge that my decision could worsen my circumstances, I decided not to pray.

There were a few others who didn't pray, including Golshan, and eventually we attracted the attention of the guards and the warden, Haji Davoud, who looked and acted like one of Tehran's traditional roughnecks. He had little education and in the course of discussions and arguments he would often lose his train of thought and end up with a blank look in his eyes. Soon after our arrival, he started visiting the unit regularly. Following instructions dictated to him from higher up, his first goal was to make all the prisoners wear hijab. Haji Davoud would pound on the unit door and quickly walk in. And from the moment he entered, he would kick and beat any prisoner within his reach who was not wearing a headscarf or a chador.

Only the Mujahedin covered themselves even when no man was present in the unit. Therefore, each time Haji Davoud entered, there was chaos as the other prisoners tore off in all directions to grab their cover. The panicked stampede created an indescribable earthquake. Suddenly, fifteen people would thrash about trying to pass through a narrow cell door.

I knew I had to cover when Haji Davoud showed up, but I decided not to go beyond wearing a headscarf, and a small one at that. Still, I was never able to fetch it in the split second between Haji Davoud's knock and his entrance, so I started to wear it tied loosely around my waist, ready to be thrown over my head the moment I heard his knock.

After a few weeks of this ridiculous game, I started to experience heart palpitations. The instant I heard Haji Davoud at the door, my heart would start beating wildly, like that of a frightened sparrow. I was thirty-five; the fifteen and sixteen year old girls must have been even more terrorized.

One night, Tayebeh, a fifteen year old guard, walked into the unit just as Golshan and I were walking out of the bathroom. For some reason she always picked on Golshan, who had been in a state of constant fear ever since Iran and Farzaneh were put to death. As soon as Tayebeh saw us, she attacked Golshan for not having any socks on. Golshan was wearing long pants that covered her legs down to her feet. She said nothing and walked toward her cell, but I suddenly realized I was shaking with rage. Tayebeh then turned to me and barked, "Hey, you aren't wearing any socks either." I looked at her and screamed, "Speak politely! You're young enough to be my daughter." The girl looked like she was about to burst into tears. I walked up to her and said, "Look here! I have nothing to say to you. Go bring someone older than yourself."

Tayebeh ran out of the unit. The prisoners were staring at me in horror. The Mujahedin and the leftists had suffered so much and had been beaten and tortured so often that they couldn't bear even the smallest incident. Everyone was begging me to control myself. My mother, who was shaking with fear, forced sedatives into my mouth. Knowing that Haji Davoud would burst in at any moment, I quickly put on my socks and covered my hair with my scarf; the other prisoners rushed to fetch their hijab as well. Minutes later, the door opened and Haji Davoud,

Tayebeh, two other guards, a few tavvābs, and a man carrying the plastic hose used for floggings walked in. I was standing in front of my cell. Haji walked up to me, but before he could say anything, I said, "You have the power to give me one lash or one thousand lashes, but it is in no way proper for a fifteen year old girl to insult someone who is old enough to be her mother. Hard as I try, I can't find any justification for insults. Besides, why do we have to wear socks at all times in a unit where everyone is a woman?"

I can't remember our entire dialogue. Of course, its only value would be to help us get to know a creature like Haji Davoud. I remember that during our argument, I moved from in front of my cell and stood facing him. I responded to every sentence he spoke. I realized he was waiting for the slightest excuse to hit me. I also knew that as long as I stood firm, he wouldn't. My mother, petrified and nervous, came and stood between us. She was a woman of great charm with a knack for understanding men, and she started to shift the conversation away from my outburst by describing her aches and pains and complaining that she needed medication.

But in the end, Haji Davoud had to do something. He turned toward our cell, pointed to one of my cellmates and said, "This one! This one has to be whipped." The girl was ordered to go over to the man holding the plastic hose. She got up and walked up to the man. Haji shouted, "Lie down!" But the girl said, "I won't lie down. It's improper! I won't lie down in front of any man."

Her reasoning had an effect on the former ruffian. He let her be and approached Golshan who was still standing in our cell. He said, "This one! Is this lady Indian? She has to be whipped." Golshan's eyes were large and had a languid look. Apparently, this had transformed her into an Indian in Haji's mind. With her head held high, Golshan walked out of the cell and toward the man holding the hose. She knelt down and covered her head with her hands.

They whipped her. It was horrible, even though part of me knew Golshan had been looking for an opportunity to demonstrate her hatred, and being flogged was in a way an expression of loathing. Suddenly Mahboubeh, who was Golshan's friend, rushed over and started to scream, "Stop it! Stop it! That's enough!" Surprised, Haji Davoud yelled, "Quiet! Shut up!"

"I won't shut up! It's enough. It's enough!"

Haji shoved her toward the door and followed her out. The guards left, too. There was total silence in the unit. Everyone was wondering what would become of Mahboubeh.

Half an hour later, she returned. She was calm. She told Golshan and me that out in the hallway, Haji had spoken to her amicably and had told her that he knew she didn't like wearing hijab, that he himself had nothing against women not covering themselves, and that she was free to take off her coverall and headscarf right there in the hallway in front of him. She had calmed down and spoken to him about some of the problems in the unit, and astoundingly, Haji had promised to help.

After that, Tayebeh became more courteous. Most surprising, she developed a sense of friendship toward Golshan, Mahboubeh, and me.

Mahboubeh's case was one of the most heartbreaking that I witnessed in prison, a reflection of the blight that had befallen our society. She was from a poor family who had all managed to better their lives through hard work. She had two brothers, one a pilot and the other a soldier at the frontlines of the war with Iraq. At thirteen, Mahboubeh had started working in a tailor's shop. A few years later, she had gotten engaged to a young university student who, after graduating, became an assistant professor. Mahboubeh, too, had continued her education while still working. Eventually, her fiancé became interested in politics and joined a leftist group. In September 1981, he was arrested and executed. On the seventh night after his death, Mahboubeh, who was utterly despondent and had been drinking, went out and aimlessly wandered the streets. A police patrol arrested her for being a prostitute and took her to the Monkerāt Committee, which dealt with religious offenses. In the minivan that transported her, a guard hit her in the face and hurled her glasses out of the window. Without her thick glasses she couldn't see. At the Monkerāt Committee they realized that she wasn't a street girl, but still they transferred her to Evin, where she was sentenced to eight months in prison, and then moved her to Ghezel-Hessar with us.

On one of our first nights at Ghezel-Hessar, when Haji Davoud visited our unit, Mahboubeh walked up close to him so that she could see his face. Haji Davoud got angry and exiled her to the leftists' cell. That was his way. As punishment, he would send the Mujahedin to the leftists' cell and the leftists to the monarchists' cell. But Mahboubeh didn't care. I think it was shortly after this incident that her family brought her a pair of glasses. Her father also brought her the collected works of Shams-e Tabrizi, Rumi's spiritual instructor, and *Masnavi-e Ma'navi* by Rumi, which made us all very happy. But I worried that a man who had the courage to bring these books to Ghezel-Hessar Prison would eventually get into trouble. The Hezbollah were frightened of color, light, scent, sound, and movement. Of course, they were not against Rumi's books, but if a man brought them to prison, for his daughter to boot, they were likely to conclude that he must be up to no good.

Some time passed and one day Mahboubeh was told she had a visitor. When she returned, she was in tears and distraught. She told us that her brother, the pilot, had been arrested in connection with a suspected coup d'état and executed. Having lost two of the people she loved most to executions, a leftist fiancé and a rightist brother, Mahboubeh grew even more troubled.

A few weeks later, again we saw her returning from a visit with her family. Now it seemed that her father had been accused of financial terrorism and arrested. I imagined that Mahboubeh's father, who was a shopkeeper, had become enraged after the execution of his son and his future son-in-law and had said things that led to his arrest, and that there was nothing more to the financial terrorism than that. Her mother was begging her to do whatever it took to be released from prison. The poor woman was caring for her executed son's two children.

Shortly after that, Mahboubeh's other brother was killed at the front. Her father had by then been released from prison and had come to bring the news to his daughter. A few months later, her wretched mother came to tell her that her father had died of a heart attack. Finally, Mahboubeh was scheduled to be released. Two days before gaining her freedom, her mother passed away.

Years later, after I was released from prison, I planned to find Mahboubeh, but I never found the courage.

DESPITE THE AGONY AND PAIN THE LEFT-ists and Mujahedin suffered in prison, and the friends and family they had lost to executions, many of them still had not grasped the truth of our situation. A large number of them still believed that the fundamentalists were ignorant and would not be able to stay in power for long. At the time, I didn't have a clear idea of what the Hezbollah were capable of; but unlike the others, I believed that they were shrewd and intelligent and that it was prudent to act as if we respected them.

The Hezbollah had gathered their forces mostly from among poorly educated rural people and those of the same background who had migrated to the cities. I came to learn that their first principle regarding anyone outside their movement was: we don't know them and don't want to know them; they should either become like us or they will be destroyed. Their attitude reminded me of the Greek myth of Procrustes who on the sacred pass between Athens and Eleusis had an iron bed in which he invited travelers to spend the night. If the guest was too short, he would stretch him to the exact length of the bed and if the guest was too tall he would cut off his legs.

The effect of Hezbollah's policies quickly became obvious.

The wealthy, the monarchists, and those who were in favor of a democracy quickly fled the country. Factories were confiscated and industries shut down. Next, the experts—doctors, engineers, lawyers—left Iran. I have heard that the government of Canada reported that the Iranians who migrated to that country during the first two years of the revolution generated millions of dollars in revenues. Strangely, despite the losses Iran was suffering, the terror continued and thousands of university professors and industry managers were purged from their positions. The last groups to fall victim to the Hezbollah were the Mujahedin and the leftists who had engaged in armed resistance and were now being herded into prison.

New prisoners continued to be transferred from Evin. One of them complained to the prison administration that there were not enough copies of the Quran in the unit. Suddenly every prisoner was given a Quran, and those who had learned how to behave in front of the guards and the warden started carrying their copy around all day. It was during this time that a so-called teacher from the holy city of Qom arrived at Ghezel-Hessar. He was an uneducated mullah dressed in the revolutionary guard uniform and he was supposed to teach an introductory course on the Arabic language. He even claimed he would soon start teaching at a university as well. I couldn't imagine what he was qualified to teach at a university, but thousands of professors had been purged so that this seed of faith could grow there. We had classes several days a week and the prisoners did well pretending they were learning a lot, but in fact most of them were better educated than the professor.

He usually arrived as we were preparing for lunch and noon prayers, which meant that the prisoners on kitchen duty would have to leave the block of ice meant for our unit sitting in the hallway. But he was oblivious and never once noticed that a large block of ice was melting a few feet away from him. It was thanks to his inattention that one day I saw a most beautiful scene: a mouse sitting on top of the ice, eagerly chewing at it, slyly looking around.

The day when the professor finally noticed the prisoners' restlessness, he said, "I know, you want to go and watch *The Pink Panther* on television!" The prisoners all smiled, a few nodded. He added, "Did you know that up until the revolution I had never seen a movie? We were told that whoever went to the cinema would go directly to hell and that frightened me. One day I ran into a friend in front of a cinema and he started talking and I stood there terrified that I would die right there and go straight to hell."

Ayatollah Abdul Hossein Dastgheib, the spiritual leader of Shiraz, was assassinated on December 11, 1981. A fifteen year old girl tied grenades to her body, covered herself with a chador, and approached the Ayatollah on the street with the excuse of wanting to give him a petition. The girl, the ayatollah, and a few revolutionary guards were all blown to pieces. And Ghezel-Hessar was suddenly flooded with the ayatollah's writings. In the introduction to one of his books he explained that certain honorable clerics believed that people should be told the truth, but that he thought it was still too soon for this and that this truth-telling should be deferred until sometime in the future. In the absence of truth, the ayatollah was busy proselytizing to the populace. In one of his books he wrote that we must wash our face in the morning because at night the devil vomits in the corners of our eyes. He also wrote that a guilty person (or perhaps an adulterer) will be cut into pieces when he dies. After his assassination, photographs of the bombing were put on display in the unit. They showed the ayatollah as having been cut into pieces.

On the day that news of the assassination was broadcast, a woman who had for some time been vying to become a tavvāb, decided to suddenly faint in shock over the holy man's death. The prisoners who still had remnants of bravery left in them ignored the unconscious woman who, true to the tradition of fainting women, lay there waiting for a rescuer to rush to her side. She lay there for almost ten minutes until a couple of prisoners decided to revive her. One of them slapped the woman hard across the face and said, "My dear, my dear, wake up!" Then she abruptly delivered another stinging slap to the woman's face. Realizing that things weren't going her way, the swooning woman opened her eyes and started to weep and cry out to the martyred ayatollah. Haji Davoud appeared and promoted her to unit manager.

It soon became obvious that Haji Davoud feared the tavvābs just as much as they feared him, and this was creating an increasingly stifling atmosphere. To make matters worse, our new unit manager, the fainter, who bore a grudge for the slaps she had received and already disliked several inmates, made our lives even more unbearable. Almost every day, she would find an excuse to file a complaint with Haji Davoud, and just like a robot he would act on the woman's suggestions. Following one such incident, she decided, and Haji Davoud agreed, that the prisoners should be locked in their cells at all times and should only be allowed to come out when they needed to use the bathroom. But this wasn't enough. Sometimes she would choose large groups of different prisoners to be locked up together in a small cell. At other times groups of prisoners would be forced to remain standing in one place for hours.

One day, when the prisoners were forbidden from talking to inmates in other cells, Golshan found the opportunity to show me her father's watch, which she had been wearing ever since she had received it, together with some of his other personal belongings. It was a large, expensive digital watch, but now it was completely shattered. Golshan looked pale. She said she had never taken it off and had not hit her hand against anything, but she had found the watch smashed when she woke up that morning. We never found out how it happened. All I know is that this strange incident had a terrible effect on us.

Soon after, two young Mujahed girls, sixteen and seventeen years old, were summoned to Evin prison. They left, carrying their belongings, looking frightened. Suddenly, I found myself in an uncontrollable state of anxiety. I took refuge in a corner of our cell. As I sat and thought about the girls, I realized that all that had been unfolding in Iran was simply because a traditional father had unexpectedly decided to punish his untraditional children, and I had been dragged into their home to witness their deadly clash. But I, and a large segment of the population of prisoners, had played no role in all that was taking place. The earthquake that had resulted from a struggle within the traditionalist segment of society had displaced everyone.

For months we had been living with the smell of blood. At a time when thieves, smugglers, and murderers were roaming free, high school and university students were being shoved in front of firing squads. As hard as I tried, I couldn't understand this method of social reform.

The following afternoon, the newspapers reported the execution of the two girls. Hours later, when I got up in the middle of the night to go to the bathroom, I saw Golshan standing in a corner, praying. I waited for her to finish and walked up to her. "I'm praying for those kids," she said. I replied, "But you oppose them." She smiled bitterly and said, "Well, that's just a political disagreement. I don't know if you can believe me or not, but I love them more than I love my father."

And again trouble and turmoil started. A talkative girl in our cell had tried to get a few cigarettes from the prison dentist and Haji Davoud found out. Although prisoners were allowed to smoke, their cigarettes were carefully rationed. At the time, delivery of cigarettes had been delayed, and the girl, who actually wasn't a smoker herself, wanted the cigarettes for two other prisoners so that she could win their favor.

Haji Davoud entered the unit and asked the girl if she was the one who had asked the dentist for cigarettes. She looked at him with horror. And the former hoodlum, his blood boiling, started to brutally beat and kick her. She fell a few times and then managed to crawl into a cell. He followed her and continued to pound her. And then, in his mad rage, Haji Davoud punched and kicked a few of the older prisoners within his reach before leaving the unit.

Little by little, this kind of punishment and humiliation intensified. Any notions about the nobleness of man had taken a back seat to the need to breed a sense of inferiority. All our work supplies, such as needles and threads, and needlepoint and embroideries, were taken away. "There is no need for you to work. You should just sit and think," Haji Davoud said. After several months, the tavvāb who had become the unit manager was transferred, and the prisoners could finally breathe easier.

Then one night, around two in the morning, the door opened and three older Mujahed women, "mothers," were brought in. One of them was unconscious from a beating. Her name was Mother Mossana. (That is her real name, and even if only one person reads this memoir, I want that person to know her name. And if Mother Mossana or her family takes issue with this, I apologize to them.)

As soon as they arrived, the two women who could walk spread out a blanket and laid Mother Mossana down. They said that that night Mother Mossana had jolted awake from her sleep and cried out, "Massoud is coming," referring to Massoud Rajavi, the Mujahedin leader. She had then grabbed her shoes and run toward the door. The guards had immediately informed Haji Davoud, who exiled her to our unit—the disciplinary unit. The two other women were sent along with her for no apparent reason.

Mother Mossana's fourteen year old daughter, who had been put in prison at the same time as her, was still in the other unit and the poor woman was constantly terrified that her child would be executed. She claimed that the girl was mentally retarded. Of course, she was not retarded at all. This was Mother Mossana's superstitious attempt to ward away the evil eye, similar to the custom of rural peasants who would spread mud on their children's head during mourning ceremonies so that they would appear ugly and ward off danger.

At night, I would sit in my cell and observe Mother Mossana. Although she had been assigned to our cell, she had spread her blanket in a small alcove in the hallway and slept there. She would lie down on her stomach, hold her head in her hands, and without making the slightest movement she'd stare straight ahead. Near dawn, when the prisoners would start preparing for their morning prayer, she would bury her head under her blanket and pretend to be asleep. She wouldn't move until noon. She loathed everyone.

One night, thinking that she must be aching and exhausted from sleeping on the floor, I went over to her and started to massage her legs from over the blanket. She said nothing and after a few seconds she pulled the blanket over her head and again feigned sleep. But gradually she warmed up to me. We would occasionally sit and talk. I was knitting a bag with strips that I had made by cutting up plastic bags. Mother Mossana liked the bag and I decided to offer it to her once it was finished. Meanwhile, I could sit with her and knit.

After a few days, she hesitantly asked whether I knew how many of her sons had been executed. I said I knew nothing about it and asked why she thought her boys had been killed. She explained that her son Ali had been arrested at the same time as she and her daughter, and that the other two boys had been taken into custody a month earlier. She said she was illiterate and had tried to find out if their names were on the list published in the newspaper, but the other prisoners had spilled ink on the page so no one could read it to her. I kept quiet. She told me their names and again asked whether I knew what had become of the boys. As far as I could remember, while I was at Evin Prison I had seen the names of two of them in the newspaper and had read the name of the third one in a newspaper at Ghezel-Hessar. But again I told her I knew nothing.

It was unacceptable to me that Mother Mossana was illiterate. She had been raised in a devout family that believed literacy corrupted girls. And to further safeguard their daughters, they married them off at a very young age. I can't quite remember whether she was eleven or twelve when they sent her to her husband's home. But she got pregnant almost immediately after her marriage. Eventually, her husband moved the family from their rural town to Tehran. There, Mother Mossana was never allowed to leave the house. Every day, her husband would buy their daily necessities and bring them home. She was even forbidden from opening the front door.

Mother Mossana was deeply depressed. Vacillating between knowing and not knowing of her sons' deaths, she was reflecting on her life, hoping to discover the reason for all the misery she had suffered. She said her husband was extremely jealous and always suspicious. Even though the woman never set foot outside the house, he still didn't believe her to be chaste. Often, he would return home at odd hours of the day to check the rooms and the basement.

Once a month, Mr. Mossana would take her back to their town so that she could visit her family. He would hire a car and have it pull up in front of the house so that she could walk out and quickly get in without being seen. After their return, there was always a storm at home. Her husband would claim that she had smiled when the driver turned on the car radio, or that she had turned and looked out the car window to attract attention. A heated argument would follow.

Early in their marriage, Mother Mossana developed asthma and suffered terribly. But her husband never took her to see a doctor because they were all men. One day, he finally gave in to pressure from her relatives and took her to the doctor. But when the doctor started to examine her, Mr. Mossana became so distraught that the doctor decided against it. He asked them to leave and told Mossana to only come back when he had accepted the fact that a medical doctor has the right to examine his patient. Back home, Mossana told his wife that he wished there were women doctors. Of course, at the time there were plenty of women doctors in Iran, but the pious man seems to have had no knowledge of their existence. Their son Ali, who was then a teenager, told his father that since he had accepted the fact that it would be good to have women doctors, he should allow his daughter to become a doctor. Enraged, Mossana beat his son so violently that the boy could not go to school for several days.

I continued to knit the plastic handbag and to think. For several years prior to the revolution, the shah's regime had been moving the country toward industrialization. Certainly, given his disposition, Mr. Mossana could not bear the changes taking place in society. And doubtless, his sons welcomed the new system. I imagined a deep conflict had taken root between father and sons. Mossana died when his sixth child—the girl who was now in the unit across the hall—was only six months old. Mother Mossana was left with the children and the equivalent of thirty dollars in her pocket. Finally, she left the house, but only occasionally, and only to buy groceries. She never did explain the source of the family's income after her husband's death. I think they were supported, in part, by religious organizations. Mother Mossana sent her oldest daughter to school but married her off as soon as she finished elementary school. Her sons tried to dissuade her, but to no avail. Sounding regretful, Mother Mossana said, "I was afraid she would become corrupt." In the end, she chose the same path for her daughter that those who had destroyed her life had chosen for her.

The Mossana boys joined the Mujahedin while the shah was still in power and were arrested. Mother Mossana joined a group of women with circumstances similar to hers. They would cook together and deliver large pots of food to the prison for the inmates. Eventually, the shah's government collapsed, the political prisoners were released, and the People's Mujahedin of Iran, thanks to the likes of the Mossana brothers, gained strength. In a film of Ayatollah Khomeini, made after his return to Iran, two of the Mossana boys are standing next to him. A clip from this film was aired on television in February 1981, after the Mujahedin had fallen into disfavor and months after the boys' execution.

One day when Assadollah Lajevardi, the warden of Evin Prison who was known as "the butcher of Evin," was conducting a lecture at Ghezel-Hessar, he suddenly asked the prisoners, "By the way, how many Mossana boys do you think have been executed?" Everyone was silent. Again he snidely asked, "How many? Do you know?" Again everyone kept quiet. Both Mother Mossana and her daughter were sitting in the group. A girl next to me whispered that when Lajevardi himself was in prison prior to the fall of the shah, the Mossana boys used to tutor his children.

Eventually, Mother Mossana was transferred to a different unit and I had little news of her. About two years later, a tavvāb came to my mother one day and told her that Mother Mossana had had a dream that worried her, and she wanted my mother to interpret it for her. She had dreamed that a man was holding on to her hands and had wrapped his legs around hers. The man's figure was round like a ball and was covered with coarse hair. The man was rolling along and taking Mother Mossana with him. At times she was under him, at times on top of him. After listening to the tavvāb, my mother said, "Tell her, God willing, it's a good omen. It's nothing important. She is emotionally tired and must rest and keep calm."

I thought the dream was perhaps an altered reflection of a guard named Brother Souri, who had viciously abused the prisoners during the summer of 1981. He had whipped many of the inmates and in a blind state of sadism had once forced Mother Mossana to crawl the entire length of the prison corridor on her chest, using only her elbows to move forward. He soon left to join the Iran-Iraq war and was killed at the front. The tavvābs held elaborate mourning services for him and the prisoners breathed a sigh of relief.

One Tuesday in early February, a tavvāb came to our unit and told Golshan that a letter had arrived for her. But they didn't deliver it to her. For quite some time, Golshan had stopped wearing her engagement ring on her finger and was instead wearing it on a chain around her neck. I had asked her why and she had said that she didn't think she would be getting married. Every Wednesday, we were allowed to go out to the courtyard for recreation and fresh air. But Golshan would usually just stay in bed. That Wednesday, eager to receive her letter, she came with us. We were in the courtyard when they announced over the PA system that Golshan should prepare to be transferred to Evin Prison. She started to walk back indoors. One of her close friends and I ran after her and cautioned her that no matter what, she should remain polite, not get angry, and not give those irrational people any excuse to hurt her.

Golshan went to the prison office and we waited outside the door. A short time later, she walked out and we went back to the unit to pack her things. A few hours after she left, a guard brought a letter Golshan had written to her family and gave it to her cellmates. It was supposed to be mailed Saturday morning when they collected our letters. On Thursday morning I woke up and saw a tavvāb from another unit leaning over me, shaking me. The girl looked pale. She whispered, "They've killed Golshan. But please don't tell anyone."

I lay on the bed and stared straight ahead. For months I had witnessed the bloodbath, but none of those killed were as close to me as Golshan. Fate had made us constant companions for six months. She was interested in reading and always eager to debate. That night they delivered our newspaper. I made no effort to be among the first to read it. A tavvāb walked in, laughed merrily, and said, "Wow! Good news! They killed Golshan!" I knew she was in fact very fond of Golshan. This was her way of concealing her horror. Golshan's other close friend, who had already read the newspaper and looked like she was about to have a heart attack, suddenly jumped as if with joy, and said, "Wonderful! So they killed her! That's wonderful!" I felt like vomiting and rushed to the bathroom. When I walked out of the toilet stall, I saw the girl standing there, trembling from head to toe and splashing water on her face. I smiled at her. She smiled back. She was trying with all her might to stop her tears from flowing.

Golshan's cellmates decided not to mail the letter she had written. They thought it would serve no purpose other than to devastate her family even more. At the same time, because prisoners never wrote anything important or private in their letters, they decided to read it. Golshan had actually written to a friend. Something along these lines, "My dear . . . I received your letter.

You wrote that you're engaged to my former fiancé and feel so embarrassed that you have even gone to a fortuneteller. I congratulate you and your husband-to-be. I am truly happy that what I have lost, you have found. Don't ever go to a fortuneteller again. It is childish. They have just now called me to go to Evin and I don't know whether I will ever return from there. But, if I am one day released, I will come to congratulate you in person . . ."

Her cellmates gathered the things Golshan had left behind and put them next to the cell door so that they could hand them to a prison officer. A few of the Mujahedin went over to take a look and one of them said, "Girls, confiscate!" And with the speed of lightening, Golshan's belongings were gone.

I watched and learned. I remembered a nationalist guerilla fighter who told me, "We stab from behind." And I thought of prisoners gathering information about each other and reporting it to the administration, which had become a common practice. I remembered the pistachios that were hidden away rather than shared . . . I remembered how, at times, human beings can be so ignoble.

A few days after Golshan's death, a young Mujahed walked up to me and said she had dreamed of her. In her dream everyone was asleep and Golshan walked into the unit half-dancing. She pranced around and disappeared again through the door. Sometime later, I heard that Golshan had been executed alone and that her body had remained lying on the ground in the execution yard for more than a day.

Golshan's death changed me. Until then, I was among the

handful of women who still went around wearing just a heads-carf instead of a chador. But with Golshan gone, I realized that in the midst of all that blood and horror, I was defending a value that at that point in time could not be defended. Most of the other political prisoners believed in full hijab or had decided to believe in it in order to get along. They considered my resistance ridiculous. And so, a few days after Golshan's death, I started wearing the thin, tattered floral chador that someone had given to my mother in Evin Prison. The first day I wore the chador, the tavvābs called Haji Davoud to come and witness his victory. I was sitting in my cell. He was standing outside the cell, smiling at me. I half glanced at him; he seemed to have the cocky command of a rooster. I stared at the wall in front of me and thought, I must have transformed into a pretty, short-legged hen. And I remembered a hen I had once seen in a rural farm. The poor thing had cuts all over and there was a large scab on her head. The other hens always went around with the rooster but this one kept her distance. "This hen doesn't like the rooster," the farmer explained, "and all the rooster's efforts to get close to her are wasted." Sitting in my cell, I felt happy, believing that even if we were transformed into animals, we could still defend our independence. I continued to stare at the wall and Haji Davoud, tired of standing there, gave the prisoners a few orders and walked out.

7 IN FEBRUARY 1982, WHILE WATCHING TELE-
vision we learned about the deaths of Moussa Khiabani and Massoud Rajavi's wife, Ashraf, two prominent
leaders of the Mujahedin. Their corpses were laid out
on the ground in one of the courtyards at Evin Prison.
The warden, Assadollah Lajevardi, was standing there, holding
Rajavi's two year old son in his arms, offering Allah's people a
report on the events that had led to the killing of the two. The
boy was staring at his mother's body, while Lajevardi caressed
him like a father.

A new group of prisoners arrived from Evin. Before board-
ing the bus, they had been taken to see the corpses. They were
hysterical. One of them, whom I'll call Feri, in a tone stuck
between laughter and screaming, described how one of the
guards had grabbed Ashraf Rajavi's corpse by the hair, lifted
her head up for them to see her face, and then let her head drop
to the ground with a thud.

Feri was a tavvāb. She was both impudent and cowardly.
Right after her arrival, when Haji Davoud came to the unit,
she rushed up to him, introduced herself, and told him she was
prepared to do anything. She had arrived with a friend, Pari,
who was always at her side. She, too, promised to do whatever

was asked of her. I got the impression that Haji Davoud didn't like them. Even though they were Mujahedin sympathizers, he assigned them to our cell.

The two girls were members of a small political faction and their team leader was said to have been a nurse. After their arrest, with the first beatings they received, they quickly gave up their team leader and led the revolutionary guards to her home. With their knowledge of the nurse's methods, they helped the guards find pieces of information tucked in the seams of her clothes and in her hair. The nurse was executed and these two were spared.

One night in Evin, Assadollah Lajevardi summoned Pari and told her that based on her promise to cooperate, she would have to take part in an execution. They put her on a minibus carrying prisoners sentenced to death. According to her, one of the prisoners was a girl who had been savagely tortured and was lying on a stretcher that wouldn't fit on the minibus horizontally. The guards finally shoved it in semi-vertically, leaving the girl's feet and the bottom part of the stretcher sticking out the door. In the execution yard, they put her up against the wall still strapped to the stretcher. After the shower of bullets, Lajevardi gave Pari a gun and led her to the girl on the stretcher, who was no more than fourteen. He showed Pari how to shoot, and she shot the girl in the head.

The two girls often spoke to the women in our unit about various incidents they had witnessed. A profound fear provoked them to seek refuge with others, and yet their dread of being executed drove them to become ruthless tavvābs. They made me unusually angry and I tried to stay away from our cell whenever they were there. My mother felt the same way and as a result, we soon moved out of the cell and settled in the alcove where Mother Mossana used to live.

Feri and Pari were running riot in the unit. They were determined to gain the attention of all the prisoners. They'd put on shows, tell jokes. One of the women, who had become aware of how I despised the two, insisted that among many political organizations it was permissible for a prisoner under duress to cooperate with the authorities and even to participate in executions. I thought that if I, too, were a member of a political organization, I might be able to accept this. But what I couldn't understand was the girls' crudeness. Their vulgar jokes disgusted me.

Feri and Pari represented a new phenomenon—creatures whose actions were based neither on remorse, nor on strategy. Fear had created monsters willing to do anything and go against any principal to survive. I hated them but I also pitied them. Feri was eighteen and Pari was twenty. Without a doubt, there are many people who would act as these girls did if faced with similar circumstances. But why should any human being be pushed to this limit?

When Feri and Pari realized that my mother and I had moved out of our cell because of them, they developed a deep resentment toward us. In the meantime, many other prisoners had started to avoid them as well. To take revenge, they picked out the youngest prisoners, all between the ages of fourteen and seventeen and complained about them to Haji Davoud. And as usual, he came running to the unit. Although none of the young girls had been actively involved in politics, they had been vocal in their partiality toward one organization or another and their schools had reported them to the authorities. In prison, they had somehow managed to keep their sense of independence and youthfulness. Haji Davoud ordered that they all be locked up together in a cell and only be allowed out for prayers and meals.

One evening I was busy knitting and stayed up all night. At dawn I saw Feri open the door to the girls' cell so that they could wash before prayers. While they were out, Pari and another tavvāb went in and dragged out their mattresses, ripped them open, and searched inside. They found a folded piece of paper.

They celebrated their great discovery with shouts of victory, which woke up everyone in the unit, and ran out. A few minutes later, Haji Davoud walked in, holding the piece of paper. He called the girls who had been locked in the cell and asked, "Who does this belong to?" The girls insisted that it didn't belong to them. Haji Davoud told them that a poem in praise of Rajavi, the Mujahedin leader whose dead wife we had just seen on TV, was written on the paper and that he would not stop searching until he put someone in front of the firing squad. Then he ordered the terrified girls to follow him out of the unit.

We had no news of them for two days. An older woman, who had been arrested at the airport because a few articles from the satirical newspaper *Asghar Agha* were discovered stuffed in her packed shoes, said that if the girls returned unharmed, she would give thanks by organizing a dinner in commemoration of her Holiness Roghiyeh, one of Imam Hossein's daughters. Eventually, the girls burst into the unit crying and screaming. For forty-eight hours, Haji Davoud had forced them to remain standing in a room and now they had to find out who the owner of the poem was or he would send all of them to Evin for a mass execution. The girls were despondent and no one knew what to do. A few minutes later, we were ordered to put on our chadors because Haji Davoud was once more on his way.

Everyone sat down in the middle of the unit. I sat to the side, leaning against the steel bars of a cell. Haji walked in and again it was all about finding the person responsible for the poem. It was obvious that he was at a loss for what to do. On the one hand he seemed to sense that the girls really had nothing to do with that piece of paper, on the other he was afraid that if he didn't punish them, the tavvābs would report him to higher authorities. He sat down, looked around, and said, "If the owner of the poem stands up and bravely confesses, I promise not to punish her."

I had found my opportunity. I said, "Haji, sir, may I speak?" He turned to me with a tired look in his eyes and nodded. "Do you remember that the day you punished these girls you took each of them out of a different cell and locked them up in that one?" He did remember. "Then, how could the poem belong to any of them? They were searched before they were put in that cell. And even if it did belong to them, they would certainly not have dared leave it there. They would have destroyed it. And Haji, sir, that would have been easy to do. All they had to do was to tear it up and have each one of them swallow a tiny piece and it would have disappeared forever."

Haji Davoud's eyes sparkled. He was genuinely happy. Then he looked pensive again and asked, "Then who does it belong to?"

"Haji, sir! This is the disciplinary unit. Many prisoners come and go. Finding its owner will be difficult. Just five or six days ago, you emptied out half the unit and sent them to other units . . ."

Unfortunately, Haji's mind could go no further. Without considering the fact that the piece of paper was frayed and old and that prisoners had come and gone in that cell for months, he ordered one of the tavvābs to go to the unit across the hall and ask who had recently been transferred out of the cell where the girls had been.

Barely a few minutes later, the tavvāb returned with two girls in tow. I was determined to intervene if he started harassing them. Haji explained to them that a piece of paper with a poem about Rajavi had been discovered and that if the owner confessed, she would be exempt from punishment. One of the girls reached out with a trembling hand and took the piece of paper from him. She glanced at it and said it didn't belong to her. Haji gave the poem to the second girl. Her voice shaking, she said, "Haji, it's mine."

"Why did you write it?"

"Because I liked Rajavi."

"Do you still like him?"

"No, Haji, sir! That's why I forgot about the poem."

Haji Davoud, having escaped disaster, kept his word and didn't punish the girl. There was joyful commotion in the unit. Oddly, Feri and Pari, who had instigated the incident, shared in the celebration as the prisoners prepared the special dinner of thanks in commemoration of her Holiness Roghiyeh.

Not long after, Haji Davoud decided to purge the books in the unit. He stood watching while a few tavvābs went to work. Most of the books were on religion and theology; of course the few novels and an English-Persian dictionary were deemed unsuitable. I think the dictionary qualified for purging because it contained foreign words. Fortunately, Haji decided to forgo taking away a book of poems by Hafiz. "Then you'll complain, 'He took away Hafiz, too!'" he said. Hafiz cast such a vast shadow that even Haji Davoud fell under his influence.

Three years later, a similar incident took place while I was still at Ghezel-Hessar. A prisoner was summoned to Evin and her cellmates were ordered to gather her belongings. The girl had been there for three years and because she had never had any visitors, she had no money. Her cellmates decided to give her some and packed it inside her prayer rug before delivering her bag to the administration office. There, the guards searched it and found the cash. The prisoner who had delivered the bag returned to the unit and told us what had happened. Everyone was nervous. Suddenly a girl named Taban said, "Tell them the money is mine."

"But, how?"

"Tell them the money was in the toothbrush cup and you packed it by mistake."

Just then one of the tavvābs returned from the administration office and started to chastise the girls. But Taban quickly stepped forward and said, "My dear, the money belongs to me. My family gave it to me when they came to visit me yesterday."

The tavvāb snapped, "You're lying."

"No," I said, "She's not lying. Just before you walked in, she was explaining to her friends that the money belonged to her."

The tavvāb believed me, and the incident came to an end. A few days later, I had the opportunity to go for a stroll in the courtyard with Taban. I told her that for the past four years I had watched how people pushed each other into hell out of fear, and that in fact, if a person was a little brave, just a little, she could protect herself and those around her. And I told her about the poem in the mattress and the courage of the girl who confessed that it belonged to her. Taban said, "I was that girl." Then she added, "But the poem didn't really belong to me." I looked at her with amazement. She said, "I'm no longer a fighter and I don't want to change the world. I just want to get this over with. That night in Solitary Unit 4, a group of girls were being martyred for nothing but a poem and Haji had said there would be no punishment. So I accepted responsibility for it. I was very frightened."

A pristine sun was shining and the sunflowers had turned to face it. I remembered that even in prison, I had at times considered myself fortunate. This was one of those occasions.

But we were not yet free of Feri and Pari's ruthless accusations. One night Haji walked in with a few guards, several tavvābs, including Feri and Pari, and his wife. The show promised to be so entertaining that Haji's wife had joined the audience.

Everyone sat down and Haji turned to the two girls and said, "Well, go ahead. Speak."

Feri stood up and called out a few names. Most of them were girls who had been involved in the incident with the poem. She then pointed to one of them and said that she had seen the girl laugh while praying. The poor girl defended herself to Haji Davoud and said that she would never mock the Quran. The others were accused of similar infractions. One by one they stood up and defended themselves. I had a feeling that this was only a prelude to the main show. And then, Haji Davoud turned to Feri and said "Well, tell us about Mrs. Vala." He was referring to my mother.

"Mrs. Vala tells filthy jokes and corrupts the mind of the youth."

My mother sprang to her feet and snapped, "Do you have no fear of God? How could you make such accusations?"

I waited patiently. I wanted to delay the moment of my own vileness as much as possible. Haji Davoud said, "Well, and what about her daughter?"

Feri said, "And her daughter is constantly walking around with everyone, injecting communist thoughts into their heads."

Haji Davoud called me. I got up and walked forward. I looked at Feri and Pari. I pitied Pari for having lost her soul by taking part in an execution and for how she was being controlled by Feri. It was unfortunate that I would crush them both. But I had no other choice.

I turned to Pari and said, "Look here, my dear girl! In the end, you have to lie in a grave just like the rest of us. Make sure you can bear the burden of what you leave behind."

Both tavvābs looked startled. Dealing with young girls who didn't have the power to talk back and defend themselves had made them impudent. Now, the weighty words of a thirty-six year old forced them into silence.

I continued, "I have kept silent. I have observed your actions and said nothing. But now, you're asking for it. My mother and I have kept out of your way, but you won't let us be. You have harassed so many people and I have said nothing because I am not responsible for defending them. But now you are singling us out and I have to break my silence."

The audience was hushed. In the absence of modern cinemas and grand theaters, they could enjoy watching how the lives of a few people stuck in prison were dragged through the mud.

Pointing at Pari, I said, "Haji, sir, this lady has taken part in execution ceremonies."

She shuddered. Haji Davoud looked at her with curiosity. I had noticed that he seemed to dislike the two girls, but because he was a partner in the game of blood and muck being carried out in the prison, he had to ally with them. Haji collected himself and quickly replied, "She has done well. I, too, would kill for Islam. I would readily kill a million people for Islam."

I said, "Absolutely. Doubtless, to defend his religion, a good Muslim could kill whenever necessary. But the problem is that these two ladies are not good Muslims. I have repeatedly stayed up until dawn to see whether they say their morning prayers or not. Once, I tried to wake them up myself. I even kicked their feet, but neither would wake up. Instead, at noon they suddenly turn into pious Muslims, put on their white chadors, hold up the Quran, and put on an elaborate show. So much so that the others who are saying their prayers with true faith and sincerity worry that their own devotion isn't absolute. Therefore, give my mother and me the right to dislike them. And that is exactly why we moved out of our cell and settled in the alcove, and that is why these girls hold a grudge against us."

Haji said he had to investigate my claim and ordered that a tavvāb who used to be the girls' cellmate be brought to him. The poor girl, who was among those trapped in prison for no valid reason and who just wanted to survive somehow, walked in. Haji asked her, "Did these two girls conduct their morning prayers?" The miserable girl said she couldn't remember and didn't know. But under Haji's relentless questioning, she finally admitted that there were perhaps occasions when the girls were tired and lapsed in their prayers. She was allowed to leave.

The game had lost its thrill but it had to continue. I said, "But Haji, sir, the story doesn't end there. The two have relations with each other . . ." Haji blanched. This was the moment when I became viler than vile and took revenge on the two girls for all that I had witnessed and experienced during the prior six months. I was adrift in baseness.

Haji snapped, "Prove it!" I glared at Pari and firmly asked, "Isn't it so?" The girl looked down. It was clear that I was right.

Haji Davoud was aghast. A show that was meant to entertain had ended up being a hard slap in his face. He shouted, "Get out! Move! Get up and go. Now!" He was addressing the prisoners as well as the group of spectators who had accompanied him. The crowd quickly dispersed. I was wallowing in sorrow. It was a dirty victory.

During the months the girls lived in our unit, I had realized that they were having intimate relations with one another. I had no issue with the nature of their relationship. But fear, an unspeakable fear, was driving them to torment others and to propel them toward death, just as they had done when they betrayed their team leader. Without a doubt, I had no right to expose their relationship. If I possessed a tiny bit of Jesus Christ's temperament, I would have taken the slap and turned the other cheek. But I was raised in a culture of an eye for an eye, and instead of observing these girls and their fear and learning from it, I divulged their secret.

I don't know what happened to Feri and Pari after that. I did not see them again until the day of my release, which coincided with theirs. Our eyes were blindfolded, though we could still peek at each other from beneath our blindfolds. We were led to the prison's main entrance. There, they uncovered our eyes. Without looking at each other, we boarded a minibus that took us as far as a nearby amusement park. We got out and still, without ever glancing at one another, we each left to follow different destinies.

8 I BELIEVE IT WAS ALSO IN THAT FEBRUARY of 1982 that the leaders of the communist Tudeh Party were arrested. They showed all of them on television. I felt I was witnessing a crucial moment in Iran's history. During much of my childhood and youth, the Tudeh Party had been extremely influential. Years later, during a conversation with a member of the party, he challenged me to "name one person in Iran's literary scene who has not been touched by the Tudeh Party." He was right. Iran's contemporary literature and translations of foreign literary works were shaped by members of the party, those who had left the party, or by people who vacillated between the party and other interests. Like many others, I too was nourished by literature that rose from the Tudeh Party. While Tudeh sought to foster the intellectual strengths of the nation, they were somewhat blind to the influence of the Soviet Union on Iran, seeing only the US as the enemy of our people. The average citizen didn't know which logic to reconcile their lives with—capitalist or communist. But during the shah's regime, the execution of some of Iran's greatest intellectuals who were Tudeh members put a halo around the party and even, to some extent, the Soviet Union.

Coinciding with the arrest of the Tudeh Party leaders,

the verdicts for those of us who had been put on trial at Evin arrived. Many were sentenced to life in prison. Among them was my mother.

I did not receive a sentence and began to write to the various officials who visited the prison, including members of parliament and the head of the revolutionary court. The letters usually read, "Respectfully, I, Shahrnush Parsipur, have been incarcerated for many months and to date have not received a sentence and am unaware of the crimes I'm accused of. I kindly request an inquiry into this matter."

As time went on, the tone of my letters changed. "Respectfully, I, Shahrnush Parsipur, have been incarcerated for two (three, four) years and have to date not received a sentence and am unaware of the crimes I am accused of. I beseech you to request that my case be inspected by all political groups. If even one person can be found to claim that they have witnessed my involvement in any political event, I will readily accept my crime. But if such a person is not found, kindly order an investigation into my situation." I did not stop writing until the day I was released.

At the end of spring 1982, Haji Davoud transferred all the prisoners in our unit to other sections. The guards led all the residents of my cell halfway down the main prison corridor when orders came that only my mother and I should return to Unit 4. By then, the solitary units in our section had been renamed, given that the term "solitary" had become meaningless when the cells housed at least twenty prisoners. My mother and I returned to Unit 4, which was now called Disciplinary

Unit 8. My mother was nervous and frightened. She missed the other prisoners from our unit. But I wasn't worried.

Before long, hordes of new prisoners arrived at Ghezel-Hessar. According to those who ended up in our unit, Haji Davoud had asked them to write a letter denouncing their political parties. A large number had done so—and the ones who had refused were transferred to our unit. Despite their refusal, it seemed to me that these were among the least ardent supporters of any political organization. They all seemed too smart to put their lives entirely in the hands of a party, a doctrine, or a religion.

A few days later, more prisoners arrived. Among them was one of the most beautiful girls I had ever seen. A girl from the Peykar Party was sitting next to me and we watched that magnificent-looking Mujahed go back and forth arranging her move. She reminded me of a short story by Chekhov. A beautiful girl boards a train with her mother. The passengers and the train staff all grow quiet. And then they all experience a certain sorrow.

The girl sitting with me said, "She is so gorgeous it almost makes one angry." I laughed.

It took only a few days for Unit 8 to become fully occupied. By September 1982 when I conducted another of my surveys, there were 298 prisoners living in the twelve cells.

During my years in prison, there were four or five occasions when national elections were held. In defense of the concept of democracy, I chose not to participate in any of them and I was not forced by the prison authorities to do so. But the political prisoners, especially those who had participated in armed resistance, were obliged to vote.

Around the time that Disciplinary Unit 8 was formed, another national election was held. On election day, two or three young girls decided to follow my example by not voting. But this was dangerous for a political prisoner in the Islamic Republic's prisons. The circumstances weren't such that I could talk to them, yet I knew that they were putting themselves in jeopardy. Therefore, I put on my chador and made as if I was going to vote. Meanwhile, a few tavvābs forced the girls to walk out to the voting area with the rest of the prisoners. The girls walked to the front of the line and I quietly returned to the unit. Later I learned that after voting, they were taken to a room and as punishment were forced to remain standing for many hours; they were beaten on several occasions as well.

After the new prisoners had settled in, Haji Davoud paid us a visit. He looked at all the girls who had gathered in the hallway, ninety percent of whom were clad in black chadors, and he sneered, "Black crows!"

I was shocked. The leftists did not believe in hijab and the Mujahedin, who always wore headscarves, tended to opt for lighter colors. But after months of wallowing in horror and suffering torture, they had accepted that they must wear black chadors. And now it was being used as an excuse to denigrate them.

The girls-turned-crows stared at Haji Davoud in silence. He

uttered a few threats and taunts and then ordered that all the new prisoners be locked up in their cells. Fortunately, because my cell was dedicated to those of us considered nonpolitical prisoners, we were exempt from this punishment. The others, however, would only be allowed out for meals and at prayer times. Each day the door to one cell would remain open so that its residents could clean the unit and wash the bathrooms.

This was the start of a difficult year in Unit 8. At first, I was terribly worried about the prisoners. It took such effort just to fit them inside their cells. Generally, seven or eight girls would sit tightly alongside the walls. Five would occupy the first bunk and given its low height, they had to sit with their neck and back bent. The five on the second bunk had the same problem. Six people would take up the third bunk, and two or three girls would squeeze together on the windowsill. Typically, two or three more would remain standing in the narrow space between the bunk bed and the steel bars of the cell. At night, they slept two or three to a bed, and on the floors.

But these prisoners possessed exceptional character. When they were let out in the evening, they would all exercise. Then the leftists who didn't pray would politely stand at a distance while the Mujahedin prayed. And the latter never behaved in a manner that could be construed as insulting by the leftists. It was a peaceful and mutually respectful coexistence.

Several of the new prisoners took a liking to my mother and me. They would often gather around us and we'd occasionally walk together. My conversations with them were generally angled toward literature, history, and most of all mythology.

They were all very young and felt the need to build relationships with older, more experienced women.

One day, a woman named Farzaneh asked me to walk with her. She was a Mujahed and a well-known prisoner. Farzaneh had been pregnant when she first arrived at Ghezel-Hessar. Haji Davoud, who at the time still had a bit of decency, was disturbed by the notion of a pregnant woman in prison and had convinced the officials to release her. But Farzaneh's husband was a ranking leader of the Mujahedin and it was rumored that the authorities released her in hopes of finding and arresting her husband. After several months, Farzaneh reappeared in prison with an infant daughter.

During one of her family's visits, she had sent her daughter to the other side of the visiting area to be with her grandparents. Haji refused to allow the child to be returned to Farzaneh. The poor mother begged and pleaded, but Haji ignored her. The next time Farzaneh's family came to visit, Haji allowed the girl to be brought over to her mother. Farzaneh picked her up and started running toward the unit, but Haji again ordered the child be taken away from her and returned to the grandparents.

The day we went for a walk, she told me I had no right to impose my political beliefs on members of her party. I didn't know why she was accusing me, but I explained to her that I was nonpolitical and that I talked about many things with the other prisoners, but never about politics. Regardless, this encounter led me again to try to distance myself from the Mujahed prisoners.

With the arrival of the new prisoners, we were seeing Haji

Davoud every day. He believed that he could break their will with his threats and punishments, and force them to write the letter of repentance and beg for his forgiveness. First he locked them up in their cells, then he banned all forms of physical exercise, and finally he tried a different tactic; he brought in a new unit manager, a timid, pretty girl, and warned us that if we ever upset her, he would make us pay dearly. He added that we were not worth even the dirt under that girl's nails.

We knew Sara, our new unit manager, from an episode of the confession series that was broadcast on the prison's closed circuit television. What she said during that one hour can be summarized as: *Like many others, at the start of the revolution my husband and I gravitated toward a political party. But he was addicted to drugs and we did not get too involved. Now that we have been arrested, there is little for us to confess to, but we will in utter sincerity confess to anything you want.*

The public prosecutor used her forced confession to argue that all leftists suffer from character flaws, such as being drug addicts. And despite the fact that Sara was one of those prisoners who would have preferred to curl up in a corner and bide her time until her term was over, the prison officials were not going to overlook their prey and forced her into becoming a tavvāb.

For several days after she arrived, Sara tried to show the prisoners that she played no particular role in any game. She stood with them in the line for the bathroom and waited her turn at meal times. Her assistant behaved similarly. On a few occasions, she even joined in the games the prisoners played during their few free hours.

But Sara was under pressure from two opposite forces. First, there was Haji Davoud who believed in breaking people's spirit and often repeated the expression, "Taking pity on a sharp-toothed tiger is cruelty against the sheep." Second, there were the prisoners, many of whom also rejected moderation and compromise because of their beliefs. Sara remained suspended between Haji Davoud's praises and the unyielding hatred of a group of prisoners, all the while trying desperately to remain indifferent to both.

By the end of that summer, the prisoners who had been locked up in their cells for months were physically and mentally exhausted. And Haji Davoud, who was now visiting the unit several times a day, looked visibly tense and nervous. It was obvious that the prisoners were not going to give in and write the letter of repentance and he was at a loss for what to do.

It pained me to see the prisoners suffering. I couldn't understand the reason for that cruel and lengthy punishment, and I could predict a bitter ending. I tried to think of something I could do to end the game. Some of the prisoners were truly exhausted, but they were in such a state that they would not give in and write the letter Haji had demanded, even if their lives depended on it.

Meanwhile, Haji took every large or small opportunity to torment them. He banned our recreation hours and no longer allowed us to buy fresh fruit and vegetables from the commissary. Once when a large tray of halva was allotted to our unit, he waited until it had been divided among the prisoners and then sent an order that we were not allowed to eat it.

One day that summer, I decided to cut my hair as short as possible. During the fifteen minutes I had to shower, squeezed in with fifteen other women in the three shower stalls, I couldn't properly wash my hair and rinse out the shampoo. Soon, a number of other prisoners also cut their hair short.

Haji Davoud heard about this and promptly showed up in the unit where he proceeded to humiliate the black crows seated before him by suggesting that the haircuts had a sexual connotation: the women who had cut their hair were playing the role of the man. I told him that I was the first person who cut her hair and I explained why. Haji was furious that he had lost a golden opportunity to torment and debase the prisoners.

One night I dreamed I was swimming in a moat surrounding an old fortress. The water was clear, yet filled with algae. I swam into the fortress through an opening and the water propelled me into what looked like a natural hot spring. I saw Haji walk by and I hid under the water because I was naked. A short while later, still naked, I was standing on top of a hill near the fortress and looking down. I saw Haji Davoud squatting next to a primitive blacksmith's shed. There was a man with him who had his back to me. In a frustrated voice, Haji was telling him, "What am I supposed to do? I'm only a poor blacksmith."

I was surprised that I dreamed of Haji as a blacksmith, because one of the older prisoners had told me that during the shah's regime, Haji had been a cook at Ghezel-Hessar and was only made warden after the revolution. I decided to ask one of the well-informed tavvābs if this was true. She looked at me in surprise and said, "No! He was a blacksmith and had a shop in Twenty-Fourth of Esfand Circle." I don't believe in the power of dreams to predict conscious life, but clearly Haji had profoundly affected my unconscious.

During that same period, I had another strange dream. I saw Haji enter our unit and, as usual, he started to accost and chastise the prisoners. I was in one of the cells in the middle of the unit, sleeping on the top bunk of the bed. I was so big and strong that I could have raised my hand and pounded him on the head so hard that he would forever be mute. But I couldn't; I was naked and couldn't come out from under my blanket.

One day Farzaneh, the woman whose child had been taken from her, came to me and said she felt compelled to tell me something but was worried that I would be upset. I assured her that there was nothing she could say that would bother me. She hesitated for a while and then said that she had dreamed that Haji Davoud had come to the unit and was preparing everyone for a new punishment. In her dream, Farzaneh felt certain that I could save everyone, but she didn't know where I was. She searched for me and saw me lying on a ledge high up on the wall, close to the ceiling. I was very large and completely naked.

I was sure I had told no one, not even my mother, about my dreams. And I was certain that I was not someone who could single-handedly save everyone. But both she and I had had dreams that shared four elements—that I could be a savior, that I was larger than life, that I was naked, and that I was in an elevated place.

Years have passed and I still think about those dreams, and I still can't find their core message. I have never been a great activist. Nor have I suffered torture severe enough to be worthy of praise for my endurance and resistance. Perhaps Farzaneh and I had similar dreams because I was an observer and I saw clearly, and I tried not to collaborate with the abusers.

ALAMEDA FREE LIBRARY

9 ONE FRIDAY TOWARD THE END OF THAT SUMmer of 1982, there was a knock on the unit door and three men walked in. The prisoners, still locked up in their cells, put on their chadors. I later discovered that one of the visitors, who was wearing a cleric's turban, was Ayatollah Khamenei's brother and, at the time, a member of parliament. Another man owned a major newspaper. I can't remember who the third man was. The men walked around the unit and ordered the guards to unlock the cell doors. The guards did so and the prisoners poured out into the hallway and sat on the floor. The men told us that if any prisoner had been tortured, she should report it to them so that they could investigate. Many eagerly walked forward and gave an account of how and when they were tortured. One woman had scars all over her body, but she sat there with pursed lips and didn't say a word. Later, she told me she thought she would be executed if she told them about what had happened to her. She believed they would not want records of their tyranny to exist. I don't know whether she was right or not. But in 1988, a large number of prisoners, some of whom had already served a long part of their prison term, were executed after standing trial. Purportedly, they were asked only one question: Do you believe in Islam?

That day, as the prisoners spoke up, the newspaper man took notes. Then Khamenei, eloquently and in true cleric fashion, addressed the crowd. I particularly remember one thing he said, "In one of the men's units, someone told me, 'I'm only upset because you removed the image of the lion and the sun from our flag.' And I replied, 'We removed the image of the lion and the sun and replaced it with the God of the lion and the sun.'"

At one point during his conversation with the prisoners, I tried to say something and he cut me off saying, "A woman never speaks up before a man!" Of course, the other women were speaking, but since I hadn't mentioned being tortured, I was not allowed to speak. A short while later Haji Davoud arrived. Mr. Khamenei turned to him and curtly said, "Leave, sir! We will talk later."

Before long, news came that Haji Davoud had left for a pilgrimage to Mecca and prison took on a certain normalcy. The girls did needlework, read books, and exercised. And then one day a tavvāb rushed in and ordered everyone into the courtyard. We stood there for a while until we were finally allowed back inside. As we entered, about ten tavvābs walked out. The unit was in complete disarray. Our belongings were scattered all over the place. The belongings of the residents of cell 1 were strewn around cell 9, and the belongings of the women in cell 9 were thrown all over cell 12, and so on. The keys to my mother's apartment that I had kept all this time were found in cell 6. All our handcraft materials had been confiscated.

In bitter silence, we tidied up. A tavvāb walked in and a handful of prisoners started to boo. Suddenly the entire unit was heckling her. Terrified, the girl ran out and a few minutes later Haji Davoud walked in, back from Mecca, with his head shaved. Everyone ran to put on their chador, but Haji started to wildly kick and beat the girls as he advanced into the unit, and he kept shouting that he would destroy us all. Finally, everyone managed to put on their chador and Haji ordered all the Mujahedin and leftist prisoners, the majority of the inmates in our unit, to go out into the section's main corridor where he kept them standing until dawn.

The prisoners were allowed back in the unit in time for morning prayers. Exhausted, everyone lined up for the bathroom. They washed, said their prayer, and fell like corpses. Breakfast was brought in and wearily everyone ate. And then they were all put back in their cells and the doors were locked. Everything went back to the way it used to be. That evening, Haji Davoud showed up again after dinner and ordered the same group back into the corridor. And thus, Khamenei's visit brought the prisoners the souvenir of a return to severe punishment. Being forced to stand in the corridor until sunrise continued for ten or twelve nights. It stopped for a few nights and then started all over again. The members of my cell would not sleep while the rest of the prisoners were standing in the corridor. We would use the showers and toilets, do whatever we had to do around the unit, and eat breakfast before they returned so that they would have a shorter wait time.

One night, I looked with sorrow at my friend, Rozan. She was a well-educated Mujahed, who was using her time in prison to practice English. Because there were no English books available, she used to hang around the pharmacy manager who would give her English language pharmaceutical brochures to read. I was teaching her the little French that I still remembered. That particular evening, she was sick and sleeping. When punishment time came, she got up and followed the others out into the corridor.

Again, my cellmates and I were awake until dawn. In the morning, when the prisoners were let back in, Rozan dropped down next to me. The girls had formed a long line for the bathroom so that they could wash before morning prayers. Rozan asked me to wake her up when the line had ended. I promised I would. She fell asleep, but every so often she would jolt awake and ask, "Did the line end?" I kept telling her that the line was still long and she would fall asleep again. Finally, I said, "Listen, Rozan, either there is a God, or there isn't. If there is no God, then there's no issue. But if there is a God, I promise you that on the day of resurrection, when you are put on trial, I will come forward and testify that if this morning your prayers were unacceptable, it was because you were sick and really needed to rest. And believe me, if God doesn't understand this, I will come to blows with him . . ." Rozan was as still as a rock and sleeping soundly.

The next night, Haji again took the prisoners out into the corridor. This time, I stepped beyond my bounds and asked the unit manager to arrange for me to meet with him. Haji accepted my request. I met him outside the unit door and we walked the length of the corridor. I told him that no one knows what the future holds, but a sound mind would suggest that we act in such a way that we will be able to justify our actions if ever we are reproached. The following day, the fiasco of standing up all night ended, but only for a brief time.

10

THE BODIES OF SEVERAL REVOLUTION-
ary guards who had been killed by members of
the Mujahedin and buried in some wasteland
were discovered, and the man who was said to
have led the attack was arrested. On the taped
broadcast on television, the man was sitting on the edge of the
grave where the bodies had been buried, with his feet dangling
inside it. He had been severely tortured and couldn't sit up
straight. Assadollah Lajevardi, the warden of Evin Prison, had
taped the event himself, but he had no talent whatsoever; he
managed to make this horrific scene seem comical, generating
laughter rather than sorrow. The death of a fish can be filmed in
such a way that it brings tears to the eyes of the audience, and
the death of hundreds of people can be portrayed in a manner
that makes everyone keel over with laughter. The scene we were
watching on television was hilarious. This upset Sara, our unit
manager, so much that she ran out of the unit. It was the first
time I saw her behave like a true tavvāb, running to tattle on us.
Soon, a man we had never seen before arrived. He sat everyone down and lectured to us. The prisoners made a few excuses,
and I tried to offer some ideas about cinematography, which
enraged him even more. Although he clearly detested people

like me, it ended only with a reprimand, and we all breathed a sigh of relief.

I think it was because of him that we were told to prepare for a prayer reading that afternoon. When the time came, we put on our chadors and sat on the floor in the middle of the unit. The door opened and a slim, tall young man walked in. His eyes were glued to the ceiling and he blinked incessantly. Instead of walking a straight line, he shuffled sideways toward the unit manager's office. We thought he was blind. Sara thought so too. She walked up to him and took his arm to guide him. But the man abruptly pulled away and said, "No, sister! I know you are chaste, just as I am." Sara quickly stepped back. The man walked toward the prisoners and sat with his back to them, facing the wall, and he recited a prayer in a heartrending voice.

A few years later when I was questioned by several inter-rogators, I noticed that they too, always looked up at the ceiling and peeked at me in between rapid blinks. I realized this was because they believed themselves to be virtuous and didn't want to look at a woman who could be another man's wife. But this very action inevitably made them constantly think about other men's wives.

It didn't take long for Haji Davoud to find an excuse to resume the nightly punishment in the corridor and to again lock the prisoners in their cells. By the end of winter and after months of relentless punishments the prisoners were tense, exhausted, and often hysterical. The physical and emotional pressures were more than a normal person could endure, and the prisoners would often behave irrationally. One time, several of us tried to find out why there were always holes on the bottom of the plastic watering cans we used in the toilets; we constantly had to buy new ones. I thought it was probably because the manufacturer was using inferior materials. I was complaining about this to one of the prisoners and the girl whispered that the holes were being made intentionally and that it was a resistance campaign. I was shocked.

"What is the point?" I asked. "We have to pay for the watering cans ourselves and we are the ones using them. What is there to be achieved by this?"

She explained that when one of the leaders of the Peykar Party, a leftist group, was being held at Evin Prison, he always tried to destroy SAVAK's property and equipment. He had even managed to meddle with the prison walkie-talkies. That was futile, I replied. SAVAK would only buy new walkie-talkies. Besides, in our case, we were destroying property that we needed and that we had to pay for.

Knowing that only a handful of the prisoners were involved in this, I told a tavvāb. The next day, Haji Davoud came to the unit and barked, "You're putting holes in the watering cans? From now on you have to buy watering cans for all the other units as well!" After that there were no more holes in our watering cans.

One day we were told to prepare for a visitor and to line up in front of our cells. A few minutes later, the door opened and Haji Davoud walked in with Assadollah Lajevardi. Haji Davoud turned to him and said, "They are the ones. They're all political." Lajevardi walked through the unit and one by one picked out a great many girls. "You! You! You, I can tell from your eyes that you're into everything! And you! . . ." He left and the handpicked prisoners were told to prepare to leave. In a frenzy, they started to pack, but minutes later orders came that they had to leave right away and many of their possessions were left behind. I later learned they were all put in solitary confinement for two to three years. And still, it was unclear how they differed from the rest of the girls in the unit. Perhaps this was Lajevardi and Haji Davoud's way of breaking the will of all the girls in the unit.

For a while, the doors to the cells remained open and then again they were locked.

And now I wonder when the strain of all those years will be released, and how it will manifest itself. The pressure is so intense that it even torments someone like me who hardly ever leaves the house.

On March 21, 1983, the Iranian New Year's Day, I had been in prison nearly two years and concluded that I was not going to be released anytime soon. I still had not learned what my sentence was, nor had I been told what I was accused of. I decided to start writing again. I asked for permission and Haji Davoud granted it, with the proviso that I not share my writings with anyone in the unit.

I wrote at night while everyone slept and put down my pen at dawn. What I was writing had nothing to do with prison. It was the first draft of a novel that I rewrote after I gained my freedom. It was published under the title *Touba and the Meaning of Night*, and it became a celebrated novel.

In early May, my cellmates and I were told that we were being transferred to a different unit. My mother and I didn't want to leave. We had witnessed and lived through painful times in Unit 8, but among the prisoners were some of the most precious people I had gotten to know during those years, girls who had fought to defend their human rights. With deep sadness, we gathered our belongings and everyone bid us farewell. After we left, the women named the alcove in the corner where my mother and I stayed, Mrs. Vala's Alley. At last, my mother had gained fame.

The girls in the unit had come to care deeply for my mother. They liked her because of her personality, her white hair, her love of reading and debating, because she tried to stand up straight and walk tall—without that slouch common to Iranians that always gives the impression that they have committed a grave sin. They also admired her attitude toward Haji Davoud, which at first was highhanded, but eventually she simply ignored him, maintaining complete silence in his presence.

One last memory of life in Unit 8:

It was dusk. The girls had been let out of their cells and were stomping their feet to get blood circulating again. It was time to watch the news on television. President Reagan and Mrs. Reagan were in the news. They were wearing formal clothes. Mrs. Reagan's gown was a one-shoulder dress made with layers of soft, delicate fabric. There was no sleeve on the right side and a round puffy sleeve on the left. The sleeve was starched and quite wide and each time she moved her arm it went up and down like an umbrella. The skirt was somewhat short and, like the top, it was layered and starched. Mrs. Reagan looked happy and was waving to a crowd we couldn't see. The girls were awestruck. I thought, one thing is certain, Mrs. Reagan is very high up and we are very low down. She doesn't see us, but we see her. That image of the young girls gathered around the television, mesmerized, has always stayed with me.

As we left the unit, our bags were taken away for inspection. Among the items confiscated were some ten notebooks of my writings. I objected and explained that I had written with Haji Davoud's express permission. But no one cared. In our new unit I often saw the tavvābs reading my notebooks and passing them around. They looked at me as if I was as insignificant as a speck of dust.

Ghezel-Hessar, Unit 6

11 MY MOTHER AND I WERE BROUGHT
to Unit 6, which was for "reformed" prisoners.
It was much larger than Unit 8. At the entrance
there was a large rectangular hall. To its right,
there was a prayer room and across the hall
was the unit's office. A door led to a very large courtyard. At
the time of the revolution, all the prison courtyards were covered with dirt. Later, some monarchists provided funds and a
few of the educated leftists and Mujahedin prisoners drew up a
plan for gardens and all the courtyards were redone with square
flower patches and blue octagonal reflecting pools.

Further into the unit and past the steel bars, the flags of
the US and the Soviet Union were again painted on the floor.
Although I had no fondness for either of these two countries,
I always tried to walk past the flags without stepping on them,
simply because I saw no logic in that stupid act. Beyond the
flags was the unit's main corridor with eight cells on either side.
The cells closest to the entrance had three triple bunk beds,
and should have held nine people. The cells toward the end of
the corridor had six triple-bunk beds, where eighteen prisoners
should have slept. However, by the time we were transferred to

the unit, there were more than five hundred women living in these eight cells.

The toilets and showers were at the far end of the corridor, and there were so many of them that it was rare to see prisoners stand on line. The sight of an unoccupied bathroom was magnificent. Just like the prisoners in Unit 8, the prisoners in this unit were extremely particular when it came to cleanliness and sanitation. The showers and toilets were washed and disinfected from floor to ceiling twice a day, and the hallways and cells were swept three times a day. The courtyard door was always open and contrary to Unit 8 where the prisoners were deprived of fresh air and sunshine for months on end, here the women could go out whenever they pleased.

Despite all this, it only took a few days for me to realize that I had been transferred from heaven to hell. Here the tavvābs lived in every cell alongside the prisoners. As a result, it was extremely difficult to have a meaningful conversation with anyone. The tavvābs outdid each other in feigning piety and godliness. Yet, hoping to gain their freedom, they took advantage of every opportunity to file complaints against the prisoners.

The women in this unit had acted more wisely than the prisoners in Unit 8, and each had written a letter of repentance as Haji Davoud had demanded. They were usually very quiet and particularly careful not to give the tavvābs any reason for complaint. They participated in all the events held in the main corridor and patiently bided their time until their release.

A short while after we moved to our new unit, the prisoners' televised confession and tell-all series started being recorded at

Ghezel-Hessar. Haji Davoud, who always tried to paint every action as having a sexual undertone, pressured the prisoners to talk along these lines. Among those who fell into his trap was an eighteen year old leftist who, after having spent a long time in solitary confinement, had agreed to confess. After explaining her political activities and admitting that her actions had no clear goal or direction, she said she had been under the strain of certain emotional needs and that each time she went to a political meeting she did so hoping to meet a particular man.

They brought the girl to our unit, where she was ostracized. The greatest disgrace for a Muslim woman is to have sexual needs and to have relations with a man who is not her husband. All alone, the girl approached me and we walked the length of the unit a few times. She said she'd be happy to learn something from an educated woman. At the time, I was studying the Taoist approach to dialectics and was trying to find its connection to Hegel and Iranian mysticism. I told the girl I was constantly thinking about ancient Chinese philosophy and eagerly explained that Hegel once wrote he had borrowed the concept of dialectics from the Chinese.

Hearing the term "dialectic," the poor girl began to tremble and said, "I'm sorry. I have things to do," before hurrying away. I suddenly realized that she thought I was trying to encourage her to join some sort of leftist political movement. The next day as I was walking in the prayer room, she and two other prisoners came in. The three sat in a corner and began talking in low voices, although I could hear that the girl's two companions were berating her for admitting that she went to political meetings just to meet a man. Visibly upset, the girl tried to explain that there were times when people might grow to care for each other. But her accusers were now shouting at her, "Getting involved in politics was wrong, but we weren't going to gatherings to meet men. We thought we were doing something good for the society. The only person who went to see men was you, only you!" I walked out so I would not have to hear any more. That night there were whispers throughout the unit and suddenly it turned into an explosion. The poor girl had tried to commit suicide by drinking cleaning detergent. They took her to the infirmary and I never heard anything about her again.

In Unit 8, despite the constant severe punishments, no one ever tried to commit suicide and no one went mad. But in Unit 6, there were many prisoners who had become unhinged. There was a mentally disturbed woman who would urinate from the top bunk of her bed. Another prisoner, while in solitary confinement, would defecate in her plate after she had finished eating and she would hand the plate to the guard. She was beaten every time. She once used her menstruation blood to write a verse from the Quran on the wall. A male prison guard was called to teach the girl a lesson. The guard had yelled, "You filthy trash, clean the wall!" And the girl had replied, "You filthy trash, this is holy blood, if it didn't exist, an animal like you wouldn't be born."

The televised confession series started featuring two new groups of prisoners. The first were prisoners who had been sentenced to death. They sat before the camera, and after explaining how they had been duped by one political group or another, they cautioned others to learn from their mistakes. The first of these prisoners ended his declaration by saying, "Some of us go down a path that ends up being a dead end. That's how it is. Always remember, 'Commit flight to memory, the bird is mortal.'"

It was a poem by Forough Farrokhzad. She had died at a young age and now, she had reemerged at the time of someone else's death. Over the next few weeks, one by one, the prisoners sentenced to death came and went.

The second group of prisoners on television were girls from my old unit, Unit 8. I was surprised at how each of them expressed remorse and repented. They were all slighting and belittling themselves. For instance, one said, "Mr. Haji, you cannot imagine what a spineless and dim-witted creature I am. Do you remember the day you came to the unit to take us away? I was so terrified that I ran and hid under the bed . . ." Another confessed, "Mr. Haji, I have spent a lot of time thinking. And believe me when I say that I am completely incompetent . . . God has made me so wretched and inept that I'm only good for being a servant in someone's house . . ."

These rantings were painful for those of us watching. For hours each day, we had to sit and listen to the so-called confessions. And the rest of our time was taken up by having to sit and watch taped lectures by a few ayatollahs, including the one who was a judge of Tehran's Islamic Revolutionary Court and was responsible for signing the orders of execution.

Despite the constant presence of the tavvābs, many of us were slowly developing friendships in the true sense of the word, even though class differences and our diverse beliefs could be great obstacles. Small things brought us together and just as easily drove us apart. For instance, every time I took a shower, I put moisturizer on my feet and then put on my socks for the cream to penetrate my skin. For some time, I had noticed that my cellmates watched me with disdain as I went through my routine. Finally, one day one of them mockingly said, "What is the sense of taking such care of your feet?" I replied, "My dear, I've noticed that you all pay attention to the shampoo you buy so that your hair will be healthy. My question is, why is hair important and feet not? God forbid, are you the type of people who only respect society's head and pay no attention to its feet where the poor are?" After this ridiculous comment, I bent down and kissed my feet and said, "My dear feet, noble and respectable, you who walk me and bear the burden of my weight, I thank you and promise to take care of you."

The prisoners laughed and in the days that followed actually began to moisturize their feet with great care and diligence.

12

AMONG THE TEACHERS WHO CAME and went, one stood out. While most of the instructors were older ayatollahs who lectured on the principles of Islam, this man, Mr. Moussavi, was a young cleric who spent his time trying to refute Marx's theories. Moussavi would doggedly push the leftist prisoners to engage in debates with him, but since many of them had repented and become tavvābs, no matter how much Moussavi rattled his saber, no one would deliberate with him. During one session, a girl asked, "Sir, why aren't women allowed to become judges?"

"Because women are weak and cannot arbitrate," he replied. "You start crying the instant you hear a loud noise." Sitting in my cell, I turned to my mother and said, "It's strange how we not only have to be in prison, but we have to bear insults and keep quiet, too."

As soon as I said this, a tavvāb who was always quick to file complaints hurried out to the unit office. A woman named Mrs. Bahmani was in the office, but we called her Mrs. Quran-i, a moniker for those who read the Quran at women's religious gatherings, because she would rather spend hours reading the holy book than speak to anyone. A few minutes later, she called me to the office and asked why I had made that comment to my mother. I explained that I considered what Mr. Moussavi said to be an insult to women. "Why didn't you say so to Mr. Moussavi?" she asked. I replied that I didn't feel like arguing with him. She insisted that I should have discussed it with him and called him to the office.

I had fallen into a trap. After months of trying to get into debates with the prisoners, Moussavi finally had his prey. He demanded that we have a debate on the prison television program. And he was adamant that we should discuss Marxism. I told him that I was not knowledgeable enough about Marxism and that he should take up the subject with more qualified people. But he would not let me be and insisted instead that we have a televised discussion about women. I told him I was against mandatory hijab and that I would only debate him if I was allowed to appear before the cameras without hijab. He laughed and said that was impossible, but agreed to let me wear a long loose overcoat that reached to my feet and a headscarf. Believing that the prison authorities would never agree to let me appear on television without a chador, I breathed a sigh of relief. However, two days later, Mrs. Bahmani called me to the office and told me that I should get ready for the debate, which would begin immediately.

I got dressed and left the unit. Mrs. Bahmani, wearing her chador, was running behind me, but I ignored her. By the time I arrived in the main prison corridor where the program was being taped, Moussavi had already started to speak and was explaining what had led to this particular session. "I was told that a lady wanted to have a debate with me, but she told me she would only participate in the program if she could appear naked in front of the camera. I said, Madam, that can't be done. You can't sit naked in front of the camera . . ."

The prisoners who made up the audience were sitting with their back to the door. I walked in and as I made my way through them, they all started to whisper. I was wearing long pants, socks, a long coverall, and a headscarf that fully covered my hair. But compared to the women in the audience, all of whom were wearing the long traditional Islamic headdress and a black chador over it, my appearance could be considered a state of undress. I walked up and sat next to Moussavi. He paused for a moment and then he pointed his finger under his chin and said, "As I was saying, if you've noticed, this part of the Islamic headdress is called a muzzle in Turkish," suggesting that women were female animals who had to wear a muzzle. And there they were, watching and listening to him.

Moussavi spoke at length. At one point he turned to the audience and sarcastically insisted that all the discoveries and inventions in the world were made by women, and that women were indeed the superior sex. Then he snickered and looked over at the men prisoners, as if to imply, Well, what can we do, they're stupid, we have to fool them. He went on for another thirty minutes defending the philosophy of Islam, the science of Islam, the growth of knowledge because of Islam, the art of Islam . . .

I sat there and wondered why he found it necessary to so ardently defend his faith when there were one billion Muslims in the world and at least eighty-five percent of the prisoners at Ghezel-Hessar belonged to political groups that strongly believed in Islam.

After more than an hour, I was finally permitted to speak. But as soon as I opened my mouth, a flood of notes from the audience came my way. All of them contained a brief message telling me that they were tired, that they didn't have the patience to sit there and listen to me, that they wanted to go back to their unit and finish their chores. But I had to say at least a few words.

"Mr. Moussavi, you said that all the inventions and discoveries in the world were achieved by women. This is not accurate. In this area, the honor often goes to men. You went on to defend Islam as a one thousand four hundred year old religion. This, too, is incorrect. In fact, Islam is a seven thousand year old religion and is closely associated with the religions that preceded it . . . Then you suggested that women are strong. It is not so. Women are fragile and must remain fragile . . . a woman's body must be soft for a child to comfortably grow inside it. If a woman's body were as hard and as muscular as a man's, two things would likely result: either the fetus would suffocate between the muscles or the growing child would cause the muscles to tear. There is wisdom to why women are weak . . . If you pay attention, the secret to creation and to creating is weakness." Then I quietly got up and left.

Eventually, Moussavi found a few leftists to debate with him. As was his custom, he orated for an hour, defending Islam and berating Marxism. Then he turned to one of the leftists and said, "You know that two plus two makes four. Now, explain why communists say two plus two may sometimes total three or five." The prisoner said that he had renounced politics and that he had no explanation to offer. But like a stubborn child, Moussavi insisted, "No, you have to say it; everyone has to hear you say it." The prisoner was quiet for a while and then he said, "You see, sir, people who are interested in such thoughts believe that space is convex and that we exist in a part of this convexity where two plus two makes four. But if we were to move to higher areas in the convex, then two and two will add up to five, and if we were to move to lower areas, then two and two will total three . . ."

Moussavi, the ninety-third generation of Adam, despite his genius forefather, possessed little intelligence. He was silent for a long time and then he quickly ended the session and ordered everyone to leave.

The Section

13 IT WAS EARLY SPRING 1984. WE HAD started our New Year celebration with a day of house cleaning. The girls even washed the ceiling and the unit was flooded with water. I suddenly saw the tavvāb who managed our cell aim a water hose at the electricity outlet. I looked at the floor, covered in water. She seemed to have gone mad and wanted to electrocute herself and kill the rest of us in the process. Several of us started screaming and she finally moved the hose away from the socket. Someone turned off the water and a few girls gently took the hose away from her. There was no point in scolding the girl. She would only run to the office and complain.

The war with Iraq was still raging and during the periodic bombardments of Tehran, I had seen the tavvāb huddle in a corner in our cell, looking terrified. The first time the city was bombed, she ran from the bathroom all the way to our cell to hide in a corner. That same girl had suddenly decided to electrocute herself.

Each time the sirens blared on television to warn of a bombing, the guards would lock the doors to the unit and the courtyard and turn off the lights. This frightened most of the prisoners even more. We had no way out if the building was hit. Still, there were those who prayed for the bombs to land on the prison.

I was in my cell, looking at the cover of a magazine. It was a photograph of burnt palm trees somewhere in Khuzestan province, a war zone. I had lived for many years in that province. I showed the picture to my mother and said, "Look at the palm trees. See what has become of them!" The tavvāb in our cell suddenly ran out and within minutes Sister Homa, an eighteen year old novice guard who had a beautiful face and utterly cold eyes, summoned me. "I'm told you've been campaigning against the war," she said.

"That is not the case," I answered. "Look at the magazine. It is published by the revolutionary guards. Seeing the photo made me sad and I talked about the burned palm trees with my mother." The girl knew she could not accuse me of being against the Iran-Iraq war, but she couldn't give up the opportunity to harass the only prisoner in the unit who didn't pray. "You feel sorry for the palm trees, but you don't feel sorry for the men who are being martyred at war," she shouted.

In recent months I had lost all patience with people like her. The tavvābs' behavior, the way some prisoners formed factions and fenced others out, being pointlessly in prison, worrying about my son . . . all of these had made me irritable and brusque. Standing in front of Sister Homa, I felt rage brew inside me. I snapped, "You are absolutely right. But palm trees didn't declare war against Iraq, the people did, and so they fight and they die. But what about the palm trees? For what reason are the poor things being destroyed?" Sister Homa was speechless.

I thought of the oil wells that had exploded in the Persian Gulf as a result of the war and said, "Lady, are you aware that the gulf is completely contaminated with oil? That the fish are dying? That if this continues the entire gulf will die?"

"So what! Let it die," the girl shot back. "If God is with us, the oil will turn into milk."

This was these people's logic. I kept quiet. But Sister Homa was waiting for her golden opportunity to discipline a nonconformist.

One day in late March, when the members of my cell were responsible for certain chores, I was put in charge of going from cell to cell at meal time to call the people picking up food for their cell. As I made my way through the unit, I reached the cell where a group of girls from northern Iran were living. They were being punished and we had been ordered not to speak to them. I walked past their cell and said out loud, "It's your turn." As I continued down the corridor, I saw the tavvāb in their cell come out and head toward the office, but I didn't think anything of it until Sister Homa came up to me and in her usual icy manner, snapped, "Why did you talk to the girls in the northerners' cell?"

"My dear, I didn't talk to them. I simply said, 'It's your turn.'"

"You should have addressed their manager."

"I wasn't paying attention. But, Sister Homa, what kind of a punishment is this? How are they any different from the rest of us?"

"Such matters are none of your business."

She walked away. A few minutes later, I was called to report to the administration office. They had me stand facing the wall for several hours until Haji Davoud arrived. He barked furiously at me, "This is it, you can't get away with it this time! You're going to the Section."

I was blindfolded, put in a car, and driven to a nearby unit. They handed me over to a tavvāb who took me to the bathroom. I was allowed to take off my blindfold. In the toilet, someone had scribbled on the wall, "I've been in the Section for sixteen months." Before leaving the bathroom, I was told to put my blindfold back on.

They led me to the Section, which I think should more appropriately be called the Graveyard. I peeked from under my blindfold. It was a large room that had been partitioned into grave-size cubicles using the same slabs of wood that made up the base of our beds. As they led me through the labyrinth, I noticed that there was one prisoner in each grave. They were all blindfolded, wearing a chador, and sitting on a bed.

They sat me down in one of the graves.

When I had been there for a while, I realized that the prisoner in the first cubicle always sat about eight inches away from the wall, the next prisoner sat at the far end of her grave and about seven feet away from the wall. The pattern continued, creating a zigzag in the position of the prisoners. I had to sit eight inches away from the wall. The daily routine in the Section was very simple. We were blindfolded all day and all night. We ate and slept with our eyes covered. The only times we were allowed to remove the rag from our eyes was in the bathroom.

Every day, we would wake up in the morning and sit in our designated spot. Breakfast would be put in front of us. This always made me feel nauseous. I was used to brushing my teeth first thing in the morning and drinking a couple of glasses of water, and I would only eat if I felt hungry. Now, I had to eat breakfast without brushing my teeth. After breakfast, we were led to the bathroom one at a time, and we each had only a few minutes to use the toilet, wash up, and rinse our plate. Then we were returned to our cubicle where we had to sit until noon. Lunch was served in the same manner as breakfast. Eating that food without water to wash it down was difficult. After the meal, we were again taken to the bathroom one at a time. Then, we were allowed to lie down until three in the afternoon. From three until dinnertime, we sat in silence again and stared at the blanket on our bed from beneath our blindfold.

The dinner ceremony was different. We were allowed to brush our teeth afterward. Once a week, we were taken to the shower room to bathe.

The television was usually on and I could follow the trial of a group of communist guerrilla fighters who had been arrested in the northern forests of Iran.

The tavvābs in the Section were mostly Kurds, and because of their lack of familiarity with the other regions of the country, they had little understanding of the prisoners. To be fair, they did not abuse the prisoners. One day when one of them was being released from prison, she stood in the unit and said out loud, "Sisters, forgive me if I have done you any wrong." Of course, given that I had never seen her face and knew that her circumstances were as precarious as ours, I silently forgave her a hundred times.

Physical exercise was banned in the Section, as was talking to the other prisoners or to the guards and tavvābs. If we ever had an urgent need to speak to a tavvāb, we had to raise our hand and wait for one of them to come over.

With blindfolded eyes, daydreaming was the only pastime. All sorts of thoughts and fantasies circled in my mind. I went on impossible journeys to the depths of the galaxy, I fixated on the idea that everything would someday end and, hence, this game, too, would have to end. I reviewed the books I had read about Nazi Germany, revisited the Spanish Inquisition, pondered the purges in Soviet Russia, delved into Arthur Koestler's personality and that of Rubashov, the hero of his book *Darkness at Noon*.

Koestler's prisons were fundamentally different from the prisons in the Islamic Republic. His protagonist, Rubashov, was not allowed to sleep so that he would become disoriented and confess to being a traitor. But his interrogator was always an interrogator. He, too, went without sleep as he struggled to get

Rubashov to confess. In Iranian prisons a group of people who had zealously embraced an ancient religion were determined to not only impose the same on others, but they wanted to force everyone to believe that they and the religion were one and the same. The truth was that they were incapable of changing anyone's beliefs. In all my years in prison, one thing became clear to me: the jailer was always inferior to the jailed. In fact, this was what led many prisoners to their death. They were not able to deny their own superiority—at least not at the moment when it could save their lives.

These random thoughts eventually led me to Taoism and the principles of *I Ching*. I was slowly approaching Buddha. I had always found it difficult to read books about Buddha and his beliefs. I never understood the reason behind this; I still don't. But a feeling always stopped me from studying him. But there, in the Section, Buddha and the limited knowledge I had of him came to my rescue. I knew that Buddha spent seven years sitting under a tree, meditating. The number seven made me feel less anxious about the length of the punishment I was enduring.

I tried to keep track of the days and dates. Fortunately, the television that was constantly on made this easy. On April 22, I was handed my belongings and, still blindfolded, I was taken to a different unit. I later learned that I was in Section 3. There, I was taken to a large room that had gravelike cubicles just like the ones I had left. I was put in one of them. During the few moments when I furtively raised the edge of my blindfold, I saw that the walls were tiled. On the wall in front of me, I saw the reflection of the window in the opposite wall and the tree outside it. I had not seen a tree in more than three years. April 22 is my son's birthday. The coincidence made me weep with joy. It's hard to believe that even in the most evil of hells there are moments of happiness. This was one of them.

For days, the memory of the tree's reflection on the wall stayed with me. Then, tedium returned. When I couldn't listen to the ongoing trial of the communist guerillas or to some other program on television, my mind darted erratically from one thought to another. I was finding it harder to concentrate on any one subject. I couldn't control my mind and this made me anxious. I would occasionally hear the prisoners crying in the adjoining cubicles. The sound was different from the usual sound of people crying. I could tell they had reached the limits of tolerance.

One night, I had just lain down on my bed when a thought crossed my mind and made me laugh. But a few seconds later, I started to cry uncontrollably. A tavvāb leaned over me and gently caressed my face and my hair. It felt pleasant, but I didn't want to be caressed. I didn't want anyone to see my tears. I wanted to tell the girl that I was not sad or upset, but we weren't allowed to speak.

Two weeks passed. Again, the fiasco of the broadcasted confessions began. A girl was speaking. She said, "My companions and I harassed one of the prisoners because we thought she was a monarchist, when she wasn't a monarchist at all. We tormented her for no reason . . ."

I recognized her voice and realized she was talking about

me. I raised my hand and a tavvāb came over to me. I whispered to her that I needed to see Haji Davoud. He must have been nearby, because he immediately showed up and I was led out to the corridor. Haji Davoud allowed me to remove my blindfold. I said, "Mr. Haji, you see, you see how they are constantly giving reports on me. It's all because of misunderstandings. Did you hear what that girl said?" He stood there for a while and looked at me with disgust. Then he wiped his eyes. I knew he was hinting that my eyes were dirty and caked with secretions. Of course, I could have snapped, You so-called pious man, what do you expect when for two months my eyes have been blindfolded with a dirty rag that who knows how many other people have been blindfolded with. But this time I managed to hold my tongue.

His reply to me was, "In the end, we will win." I didn't know what he meant, but I assumed some other faction inside the government was gaining power and rising to the surface. I said, "I don't know, Mr. Haji. Our times come with many games. Perhaps you will win. Perhaps the monarchists will win." A Mujahed girl in a chador was walking by. I motioned toward her and said, "Perhaps they will win."

That day, Haji allowed my mother to visit me. I was taken out to the corridor where we spent a few minutes talking. A few hours later, Haji ordered that I be returned to my old unit. The prisoners seemed happy to see me. But I was depressed and a bit disoriented; I remained that way for a long time. When I went to take a shower, I noticed everyone staring at me. A friend who was in the bathroom exclaimed, "My God! You have become so thin!"

I was surprised. While I was in the Section, I ate more than I usually did. Normally, I never ate breakfast, because we had so little physical activity and I didn't want to gain weight. In the Section, I ate breakfast and had no physical activity at all, but still I lost weight.

Several days after my return to the unit, word spread that inspectors from some international organizations were coming to visit Ghezel-Hessar. A few of the prisoners encouraged me to find an opportunity to speak to them. I remembered the tortured woman who had kept silent when Mr. Khamenei visited us and asked those who had been mistreated to speak up. I decided that if the visitor who came to our unit seemed to be someone important, I would speak to him, otherwise I would not risk Haji's wrath. That same day, Sister Homa showed up in the courtyard looking upset and nervous. She kept hovering around me. Finally, she approached me and said, "I am leaving. Absolve me of any ills I may have done to you." I shook her hand and told her I had no resentment toward her.

I wasn't being completely honest. But I didn't say this out of fear. It was clear that in the course of certain events, Haji Davoud and his underlings had fallen from grace. Later, thinking about shaking her hand always made me angry at myself. It would have been enough if I had just nodded and walked away.

With the shift in power, the prison was being restructured

and reorganized. Along with many others, I was moved to a different cell. This time, the tavvāb in charge of my cell was a former member of an extremist leftist group. In prison, she had discovered faith and embraced Islam.

A girl named Forutan, who had also been a member of an extreme leftist group, was brought to our unit. I had first met her in Unit 8. She was among the girls whom Assadollah Laje-vardi had handpicked and led out of the unit. They had spent all this time in solitary confinement.

When I saw her, Forutan smiled at me and walked over. We kissed each other on the cheeks and she said, "I have to confess, I'm in love, and I'm not ashamed of it." I was stunned. I wondered why being in love would make anyone feel ashamed, until I realized that like many leftists, she probably didn't know how to deal with love and being in love; most Iranian leftists were so preoccupied with the notion of fighting and saving mankind that many considered a love relationship nothing but a distraction from their sworn mission, and even immoral.

And who could she be in love with? She had spent months in a solitary cell. Had she fallen in love with a guard or an interrogator? Had she been to the infirmary and fallen in love with one of the doctors?

I said, "Love is something to celebrate. I congratulate you. It is every human being's natural right to fall in love."

And then she said, "I'm in love with Mr. Washcloth."

Forutan went on to explain that one day when she climbed up on the radiator in her solitary cell to hang clothes she had washed on the window bars, she looked out and saw a man's hand waving to her from behind a small window in the unit across the courtyard. She waved back. The man's hand signaled that he would wave to her again in one hour. Little by little, a relationship developed between them. The man would always hang a washcloth from his window bars fifteen minutes before they were to communicate. If the washcloth wasn't there, Forutan would know the man was not alone. Gradually, they invented their own sign language and sometimes spent hours conversing. I don't know if she ever found out who Mr. Washcloth was, or if she even saw his face.

14

TIME PASSED WITH NO SIGNIFICANT events. We didn't know much about the changes that were taking place in the prison and its administration. The guards and security personnel who could leak news from the outside had all gradually been replaced by tavvābs who, like us, had no contact with the outside world. Our only source of information was the closed circuit television.

One day the tavvāb in our cell announced that there would be a meeting at three o'clock and that all cellmates should be present. At the meeting, she claimed that some of the girls had complained that because I didn't pray, I was impure and unclean and therefore it was not appropriate for me to eat with them or to wash their dishes when it was my turn to do chores. My mother flew into a rage. She sprang up and spoke furiously for almost forty-five minutes. I can't recall everything she said, but I do remember one comment. "The day God weighs our actions, he will make you carry my daughter's coffin into heaven!" The prospect of having to be carried to heaven in a coffin troubled me.

I patiently waited for my mother's fury to ebb. Finally, when she paused for a moment, I said, "Please, allow me! I'm old and wise and can defend myself." Then I turned to my cellmates and the tavvāb and I said, "Friends, I accept your fatwa and, of course, from now on I will separate myself from you . . . Today, I am here because I am forced to be here. But tomorrow when these doors open, I will keep myself millions of light years away from you. Because I too consider you filthy and unclean . . ."

Except for the tavvābs, the girls all looked shocked. They had patiently and quietly bided their time in prison and did their best to not get dragged into the various games at play. I could see how my words had hurt them. But at that moment I wasn't able to show them, even with a wink, that my words weren't directed at them.

From that day on, I ate apart from the others. It was an advantage. While everyone had to wait their turn for food, I went directly to the person in charge and often received a healthier portion than the rest of the prisoners. This upset a few of the tavvābs. Also, for me to not contaminate anything, I was excused from any duty that involved water. I no longer had to clean the bathrooms and toilets, and in our cell, I was only assigned "dry" chores.

On a hot afternoon in the middle of summer, I was in our cell. I was thirsty. I picked up the carafe to pour a glass of water. The carafe was filled with ice and its outside had sweat. The tavvāb in charge suddenly snapped, "Excuse me! You shouldn't have used that carafe, it's wet and by touching it you have contaminated it." I replied, "You are right. I won't touch it again."

After more than three years in prison, I was exhausted. After lunch, I went to one of the managing tavvābs and asked her out into the courtyard. I said, "Look here, my dear. You are either truly a tavvāb or you still believe in your politics and are pretending to have reformed. I don't care either way. But what I am about to say is what I can say verbatim to Mr. Lajevardi or to any other official, so I suggest you listen carefully."

The girl looked nervous. I continued, "From the first day I was put in this prison, until this very moment, I could have done things to secure my release. Do you know why?" She shook her head. "You are all younger than me and haven't seen as many movies and plays as I have. All I need to do is snitch on a few of you so-called tavvābs. And why shouldn't I?" The girl looked like she was about to faint. I said, "I can tell by the way you smile at each other, by the way you gesture to each other, by the way you whisper, who is pretending and who is not."

The girl continued to walk next to me like a sheep. I felt sorry for her. I pitied this lost generation, many of whom had been among the brightest students in the country. I remembered a poem by Tao Te Ching, that loosely translated, said, when the horses were free, they galloped across the plains, and when anger simmered, they bit each other . . . they turned cunning the day their necks were bridled and their backs burdened . . .

I went on and told the girl that I had kept my silence because I wanted to leave prison knowing that I had hurt no one, that as a writer I needed to respect certain boundaries, otherwise my pen would go dry. But, I added, that that didn't mean I believed in turning the other cheek. I ended my talk by warning her that if one other tavvāb ever interfered with me again, I would do what I had to.

A few days later, one of the tavvābs stood in the unit's main hallway and addressed me in a loud voice, "Last night I dreamed that you were praying. I was surprised, but then a voice said to me, she has always prayed, you just haven't seen it."

I think the tavvābs reported three dreams in which I was praying. And life in prison continued.

15 THE PRISON'S CULTURAL DEPARTMENT organized a book fair. On our day to go to the fair, the girls quickly put on their chadors and rushed over to the main prison corridor. They raided the display tables as if the most expensive department store had announced the greatest sale. It was pandemonium. While I was browsing, one of the brothers from the cultural department approached me and asked why I was not participating in the story writing class they were holding in my unit. I had heard from one of the girls who attended the class that one of the teachers had described stories written by me and another Iranian writer, Sadeq Chubak, as "vulgar." I didn't tell him that; I merely said that I was too old for such things and that it was better for the younger women to benefit from them.

The next day, there was total silence in the unit. Everyone was reading. I enjoyed our blessed right to read. Now, we had a few nineteenth-century classics, *War and Peace*, *Great Expectations*, and I took great pleasure in reading *The Upanishads*. Prior to the book fair, the only books in the unit had been a few battered texts on Islam and theology and different translations of the Quran. Reading the Quran, I had come to the conclusion that, depending on the translation, the holy book could be interpreted differently. The translation I liked most was by Seraj, a Muslim writer and scholar. On one page of his edition, in the margin, there was a notation that when the principles of prayer were first being established, the Prophet of Islam would pray while standing on tiptoe. But when he realized that this would be difficult to do for his followers, he ordered them to pray with their feet flat on the ground. Reading this made me respect that eminent man even more. Great men feel obliged to live by the principles they devise before they demand it of others.

The changes the cultural department was bringing about even resulted in my notebooks being returned to me. One day I was summoned to meet with an investigator. As I walked toward the infirmary, where the interview would take place, I passed several tavvābs. They were watching me with apprehension. I realized they were afraid of what I would tell the investigator about them. I thought I should smile and ease their worry. But I chose instead to feign a menacing look. The girls were terrified. During my meeting, they constantly walked into the infirmary pretending they had to fetch something or put something back.

The investigator told me that he and several others had reviewed the ten notebooks that had been taken away from me when we left Unit 8. He apologized and said he saw no reason why they should not be returned. Then he asked if there was anything else he could do for me. I explained to him what I had explained to so many others: that I had never been involved in politics and that I had spent years in prison without having been accused of a crime and without having been sentenced.

I told him that at fourteen I was taught to offer a firm hand-shake and to smile when I met people. Now, it was difficult for me to do the opposite—to never shake hands with a man, to not smile, and to consider this polite behavior. I told him I was taught that women should always walk ahead of men. Now I had trouble doing the opposite. I told him I hated being forced to wear hijab, that I could not bear it. And in the end, I told him that my watch was broken and that a visitor had brought me a new one, but the prison administration would not let me have it. He said receiving a watch was against regulations and that if I needed to know the time, I should look up at the wall clock in the unit.

He kept encouraging me to talk. I suppose he expected me to tell him about what went on in the unit. If he had displayed the smallest sign of compassion, I could have told him how cruelty and oppression had changed the prisoners. How fear had created complicated behavior patterns and deceptive relationships. How, one cowardly tavvāb would save herself by pointing the finger at another. And the one she blamed, who well understood the rules of the game, was compelled to tattle on yet a third, who, to protect herself, exposed a fourth. And how I was the easiest target for all of them: I didn't pray, I was against mandatory hijab, and among all those believers in different ideologies, I was the only one defending the vanishing notion of democracy.

I could have told all this to the investigator. But he would then demand that I name names, and doing so would only result in girls being sent to solitary confinement, receiving lashes, and even losing their lives. And so I said, "Recently, they asked us to make a list of pastries we'd like. But they still haven't delivered them. This isn't right." He looked at me with contempt. Perhaps he was wondering how a writer could be so petty.

I returned to the unit. I spent a few days reading the notebooks that had been returned to me. In one of them, they had ripped out two pages in which I had described the burial ceremony of a fourteen year old girl, a scene I would later use in *Touba and the Meaning of Night*. All the while, I was thinking that this new phase of moderation and leniency would end if a more extremist faction were to gain power in the government. I was thinking I should burn the notebooks. If time and life allowed, I could rewrite that novel.

A few days later, the cultural department told me they could provide books for me to translate. I respectfully declined. I couldn't understand why they thought I would want to serve the very people who had kept me in prison all these years.

In fall 1984, I learned that my mother and I were among those who had been granted clemency. My mother was the first to be summoned to the prison administration office and told she was being released. When she brought the news back to the unit, I was surprised at the jubilation. The girls were tossing my mother up in the air and screaming with joy. My mother, weeping uncontrollably, gathered her belongings, bid everyone farewell, and left. An hour later, she was back. The prison officials had changed their mind.

Another two months passed, and finally my mother was truly set free. On the day of her release, she was told she had to agree to a televised interview, during which she would admit that she had been an active member of a political faction. My mother, who was naïve in such matters, agreed. During the interview, she casually said, "I was arrested in connection with little factions." And with these few awkward words, she helped the revolutionary court justify the three and a half years she had spent in prison.

Weeks went by and I was still waiting to be released. I couldn't understand the delay. While I waited, one day, for the very first time, school textbooks were delivered to the unit. The younger girls, who had been deprived of their education for three years, started studying, and the older university and high school students took on the task of tutoring them. I asked permission to teach French. Permission was granted, but I was only allowed to teach one student at a time. There was one copy of Mauger's *Cours de Langue et de Civilisation Française* in the unit. The girls started making handwritten copies of it. Teaching French one student at a time was exhausting and made little sense, but it kept me busy. In May, the girls took the standard final exams for their school year. Several passed with a grade of nineteen out of twenty.

Little by little, case files were being reviewed and some of the prisoners were being released. It was all part of the reforms taking effect under the direction of Ayatollah Montazeri, a member of the Revolutionary Council who had been named deputy to Supreme Leader Khomeini. Ayatollah Montazeri's son-in-law, who was also a cleric, became a regular presence at Ghezel-Hessar and often gave talks in the main prison corridor. In one session, he suggested that Haji Davoud was not only a cruel man, but that he was insane. In fact, we had not seen Haji for some time.

Although these were supposedly more moderate men in power, much remained the same. In the summer of 1985, one of the leftist girls was badly beaten and tortured. When they returned her to the unit, she was unconscious. She had been punished for going to meet a prison official while wearing a regular chador instead of a black one, which all political prisoners had to wear. I asked her, "What value does a regular chador have that you risk so much to defend it?"

"It's the dress of the people, not that of the Hezbollah," she answered.

"When these people are overthrown, will you still wear a chador?" I asked.

"No."

"Then it's insignificant and not worth defending."

The following day, I was summoned by the manager of our unit and told that the prison administration had decided that all women must wear black chadors. I assumed one of the tavvābs had overheard our conversation. I could no longer risk my life for a piece of fabric that symbolized nothing but slavery and servitude. I asked my family to buy the cheapest, shoddiest, and most repulsive piece of black fabric they could find and to make a chador for me. I told them I would never wear it anywhere other than in prison. I would even forgo visiting my father's grave, which was my greatest wish, if it meant I had to wear a black chador to go to the cemetery.

Several months passed. I had now spent more than four years in prison, and still there was no indication of the clemency I had been told I had received. I was psychologically exhausted and had started experiencing emotional outbursts.

Then one day I was told to prepare to be transferred to Evin Prison for my release. My friends gathered around me, and fully aware of my fragile state of mind, they made me take a few sedatives and put a few more in my pocket.

At Evin I was put in a solitary cell. They had taken my belongings from me and I found that I needed something. I called to the guard and when she opened my cell door, I said, "I'm sorry sister, but would it be possible . . ." Before I could finish my sentence, the girl shouted, "Shut up, you piece of trash! You're all driving me crazy. Why won't you idiots leave me alone?" And she slammed the door shut.

For four years I had been trained to transport myself to a time several centuries earlier, to behave "traditionally." And so I raised my eyes to the ceiling, beat my fist on my chest, and screamed, "I wish with all my heart that you drop dead!"

Then, completely disorientated, I crouched in a corner. What had I become? All my life, I had tried never to curse, never to gossip, never to make snide remarks. And now I had wished death for a girl who was young enough to be my daughter. And yet I wasn't sorry. I was in that sanctified dimension unique to oppressed people. Under duress, you create a great "I" of fantastical strength. You come to believe that you have the power to damn someone, or that with your glare you can destroy your oppressor's peace of mind.

The next day, I was blindfolded, taken to the prison's central building, and left to sit in a corner. I had taken a few sedatives. There were several women there who had been arrested at a wedding reception. It was common for the revolutionary guards to raid weddings and parties and to arrest people for listening to music, dancing, drinking, and for being in the company of the opposite sex—unless the host was wealthy enough to have bribed the local patrols.

The women appeared to be well-off and I wondered why they hadn't paid off their local patrols. A prison guard, who I knew from my days at Evin, was questioning them. The guard was a simpleminded woman who delighted in gossip. At the time of my arrest, she had been in her mid-thirties and still single. The prisoners, knowing that her greatest wish was to get married, constantly told her that they were praying for her to find a husband and this made the gullible woman happy. Later, I saw her at Ghezel-Hessar; by then she had married. I asked her, "How old is your husband?"

"Twenty-six."

Given their age difference, I understood her circumstances. "Does your husband have another wife?" I asked. Her smile faded. "How old is his other wife?"

"Twenty-two. But, you know, she isn't a revolutionary."

"What do you mean?"

"Well, she wears a regular chador and her hair is always showing. And she goes out on the street looking like that."

Since the guard *was* a revolutionary, every month, in addition to her salary, she received a large sack of rice and a large can of cooking oil from the government. Thanks to the revolution, she even had enough money to buy a house. And so it was easier for her to find a husband and to put up with a twenty-two year old rival wife who was probably beautiful.

And now here she was, interrogating the wealthy women. "How many guests were there? Were you dancing? Whose dress was the prettiest? What did they serve for dinner?" The women answered her questions but with increasing insolence, and finally the guard told them to be quiet. But they continued to talk. She stormed out and returned with a male guard. "I keep telling them to be quiet, but they won't listen to me." The man kicked the women a few times, demanded that they keep quiet, and left.

Finally, I was taken to see the judge, an old cleric. He asked the same questions I had been asked many times before. Under the influence of the sedatives, I calmly replied to all of them. They took me back to Ghezel-Hessar Prison, to my old unit.

My mother came to visit me. I took an embroidery I had completed with me to the visitor's room. I wanted to give it to her to take home. The guard at the door asked, "Do you have anything on you?" I could not bear more secrecy and games. I said, "Yes, I have a piece of embroidery." He looked at it and said I needed permission to give it to my mother, and he took it away.

I had worked hard on it. The fabric was navy blue. The design was a woman who had emerged from the middle of a water lily. Her hair was entirely made up of tiny stars. She had six arms and in five hands she held a different tool—a caliper, a hammer, a sickle, a sword, a balance. In the sixth hand, she held a chalice of wine. At the bottom I had embroidered a verse by Hafiz, the fourteenth-century poet beloved by all Iranians:

If you drink wine, sprinkle a sip on the earth
Dread not the loss from which another will gain

After I was released from prison, I went back three times to try to get that embroidery. On my third visit, a prison employee brought it to me and asked, "What does this mean?" I explained, "It symbolizes man's work. Women give birth to men, men work and build tools. If you pay attention, you will see that most of the woman's hands look masculine."

He scrutinized the design and finally said, "No, unfortunately we can't return this to you. It is confiscated."

I have lost much in my life, but after all these years, I still cannot forgive these people, and I still regret why I didn't lie when the guard asked, "Do you have anything on you?"

And now I waited for my release. I spent my time walking around the courtyard and thinking about all my years in prison. I recalled a memory that has always made me happy. We had been sent out into the courtyard so that a few of the men prisoners could come and repair the shower stalls in our unit. When they finished their work, we were allowed back inside. I had just walked into my cell when I heard loud cheering coming from the bathroom. I walked over and made my way through the crowd that had gathered. The shower stall floors had always been coated with cement, but the men had tiled the floor of the stall that was used exclusively by the children in the unit. The women were jubilant.

During the remainder of my days in Unit 4, Section 3, of Ghezel-Hessar Prison, no one other than the children and their mothers ever took the liberty of using that shower stall.

I remembered a small boy in the unit who always reminded me of Saint Exupery's *Little Prince*. Ahmad-Reza was thin and delicate. Haji Davoud had granted permission for him to occasionally visit his father who was also an inmate at Ghezel-Hessar. Growing up surrounded by women, Ahmad-Reza knew nothing about men and their world. After returning from his visits with his father he would often say things such as, "Dad's friends are mean and they all have hair on their face." Whenever the women asked him to pray, Ahmad-Reza would quickly pull a chador over his head and go through the motions of prayer.

On March 19, 1985, I was once again told to pack my belongings. My friends and a group of other prisoners gathered around to say goodbye, believing that this time I would really be released. We kissed each other on the cheeks and I left. I was blindfolded and taken to the prosecutor's office. They left me sitting on the ground in a hallway for several hours. It was dusk by the time they came for me and took me to an office. An administrator told me that someone had offered a security for my release. He put a piece of paper in front of me and asked me to sign it. The sheet had my name and other information on it, but there was nothing written in front of the heading "charges." I said, "I won't sign this. 'Charges' has been left blank and later you can write whatever you like there." He said, "Write anything you want." I took the pen and drew a straight line across "charges" and signed the document. Later, I regretted that I didn't write "charged with no crime," even though by then I knew that these documents were easily doctored.

I was put on a minibus and driven to the parking lot of an amusement park. Pari and Feri were on the bus also. My family was waiting for me. We went home and after four years, seven months, and seven days, I kissed my son.

Tehran

16 I SPENT MY FIRST FEW MONTHS OF freedom visiting friends and relatives. And then, life showed its ugly face. The family was in financial ruin, and now with years wasted in prison and at a time when the country was at war, I had to find a way to earn a living. I tried to find a publisher for the books I had written before the revolution—*The Dog and the Long Winter* and *Women Without Men*. But the publishers were afraid of working with a writer who had just been released from prison. Only one publisher, Noghreh Publishing, agreed to try and publish *Women Without Men*.

Ever since the Islamic Revolution, publishers have been obliged to deliver a manuscript of the book they hope to print to the Ministry of Culture and Islamic Guidance. If the manuscript meets with the ministry's approval, the publisher receives a permit to print the book. Mohamad Reza Asslani, Noghreh's publisher, delivered my manuscript to the ministry, and then we waited. Months later, he called to tell me that the ministry had made its decision and that it would be better if I went there myself to pick up the manuscript. At the ministry, a gentleman gave me the manuscript and told me they would allow the book to be published if certain segments were deleted. I agreed to do as he asked, and left.

I deleted all the sentences and phrases they had underlined, retyped the manuscript, and gave it to Mr. Asslani. Almost a year later, his wife returned it to me and told me they had reached their quota for the year and, for the time being, they were unable to print the book.

Since I couldn't count on any income from books, I turned to translation. I decided to translate a four-volume book on the history of China from 1848 to 1948 and went to see the publisher who years earlier had published my translation of a book on Chinese astrology. He had been profiting handsomely from it. He agreed to publish the history book and I went to work on the first volume. I spent most of my days translating and the rest of my time standing on long lines to buy government subsidized meat, rice, and cigarettes. One day I stood on line for fish from seven in the morning until two in the afternoon. The family finances did not allow us to shop in regular stores.

Toward the end of the summer, a friend who was looking to lease out a property that had recently become vacant, suggested I use it to set up a bookstore. Another acquaintance volunteered to become my partner. The space was in a basement on Sanaii Street, not really suitable for a bookstore, but I thought perhaps through word of mouth I could gather a regular clientele and also create a gathering place for intellectuals.

My partner and I went to work and with hardly any capital got the store up and running as quickly as possible. Two months later, my partner decided she no longer wanted to own a bookstore. I sold the only piece of gold jewelry I still had and settled our account.

It was a grueling time. I was shouldering much of the responsibility at home, running the bookstore, and had started working on my novel—*Touba and the Meaning of Night*. Meanwhile, I had finished translating the book on Chinese history, but the publisher was no longer interested. To make matters worse, as a condition of my release from prison, once a month I had to report to the Islamic Revolution Committee to answer a series of nonsensical questions.

During my years in prison, I had often thought about leaving Iran. But after my release, this was no longer feasible, since the government would not issue me a passport. My son, who was still in high school, was becoming eligible for military service and he wouldn't be able to get a passport either. And I didn't have the money to pay for fake travel documents. What's more, I still believed that to be able to write, I had to stay in my homeland.

I was haunted by memories of prison. I often thought about doing something to honor the memory of the women and girls who had lost their lives there, but I knew anything I did or wrote as a tribute to them would put me in jeopardy. I was in a fragile emotional state and suffered from deep anxiety. I felt terribly alone and craved a romantic relationship. But fear of being followed and of being accused of promiscuity and adultery made me give up on the idea of finding a companion. Still the fantasy of leaning on a man was constantly in my thoughts.

There were very few customers at the bookstore, but I was afraid of encouraging friends and acquaintances to come there. I didn't have the courage to do any sort of advertising at all. I continued to borrow money to keep the store open.

In March 1987, when I went for my monthly visit to the Islamic Revolution Committee, I filled out the same questionnaire they handed me every time. Next to the word "occupation" I wrote "bookstore owner." The investigator wrote, "To cooperate, please list the names of the people who frequent the store." A wave of rage suddenly surged inside me. This had been happening with greater frequency since my last few months in prison. Trying desperately not to lose control, I wrote that I was not a spy to offer them a list of my clients. The investigator dismissed me. I returned to the bookstore and decided to shut it down. I didn't want to risk the lives of others simply because I needed to make a living.

That spring, I decided to try and meet with a government official to find out if the authorities would continue to impede my efforts to publish my work and earn a living. I went to see Gholam Ali Haddad-Adel, who was minister of education at the time and the only member of Hezbollah whom I knew. He had been a student of physics and philosophy at Tehran University at the same time as I was studying sociology there. I was granted an appointment.

During our meeting, he was polite to me. I explained that I had spent years in prison for no reason, that I had to report to the Islamic Revolution Committee once a month, and that in my present emotional state I could not continue doing so.

I told him that I was a socialist, that I believed in democracy, and that I hated mandatory hijab. I added that I wished he would clarify these points for the public prosecutor's office so that perhaps they would stop harassing me. I went on to tell him that I wanted to work. I had taken with me the first volume of the Chinese history book. I showed it to him and told him that I would willingly cooperate with a governmental or semi-governmental organization to publish it.

What I was doing went against all that I believed in, but I thought my offer to cooperate would put an end to the persecutions. Sitting in Haddad-Adel's office, again a sense of fury suddenly came over me. This time, I could not control it. I started to weep uncontrollably, and to counter this display of weakness, I started to scream. Unfortunately, there was no one knowledgeable enough in my life to recognize that I was suffering from a psychological illness and that I needed medical treatment.

Haddad-Adel tried to help and introduced me to an Asian Islamic organization. It was now under the supervision of Ayatollah Khomeini's son-in-law. They agreed to publish the Chinese history book. With great reluctance, I started going to the center regularly to work on the project, even though I often found myself in the company of a young employee who took every opportunity to harass me.

One morning, I went to Evin Prison for what was supposed to be my last monthly visit. During the meeting with the investigator, I again experienced a state of rage and madness. And in the end, I was told that I had to continue with the monthly visits. Distraught, I returned to work only to discover that the young man who had been tormenting me had forged my signature under the signature of the center's director on an important document, giving the impression that I was vying for the director's position. I confronted him and said, "Look here, I've just returned from Evin where all they want is for me to cooperate with them. Do you want me to go back there right now and tell them that you are forging signatures and that perhaps you have even forged the director's signature many times?" Looking terrified, he tore up the letter.

I was exhausted. I struggled to finish writing *Touba and the Meaning of Night.* Finally, an Iranian engineering company for which I was occasionally editing and translating documents from English into Persian offered me a full-time position and a decent salary. In three months I translated two books for them: *Manufacturing Prefabricated Cement Structures* and *How to Install Prefabricated Cement Structures.*

War with Iraq continued to rage. By early March 1988, three years after I had been released from prison, Tehran was under regular, heavy bombardment. The city emptied as people took refuge in the countryside. The engineering company had little work and no need for a translator. My employment ended.

A few weeks later, I reported to Evin Prison for my appearance at the Islamic Revolution Committee. As usual, the investigator had me write down the answers to a series of questions. When I finished he scribbled "next appointment" in my file and put in a date a month away.

"I won't come," I said.

"You have to."

"I won't."

"Then I will have them arrest you right now."

"Do whatever you want. I will not come here again."

I lost control. I burst into tears. I screamed. I shouted. Everyone was frightened. They quickly took me into a room and closed the door. I was talking hysterically; I couldn't stop. I only remember some of what I said: "I'm tired of seeing revolutionary guards. The moment I see one, I get sick. I'm going to go to Sweden, to the north. I'm going to live in an igloo. So what if I freeze. At least I won't have to see another revolutionary guard or bearded man ever again."

It was true; walking down the street, I turned away each time I came face-to-face with a revolutionary guard or a "sister" clad in full Islamic hijab, so that they wouldn't see the hatred in my eyes. Men with beards or stubble on their face made me shudder.

I was ranting. I was rude and insulting, but the investigator realized that I was at my rope's end and emotionally troubled. He put some papers in front of me to sign and said I would not have to come back again. After seven years, I felt as if I could finally breathe.

I finally finished writing *Touba and the Meaning of Night* and found a publisher, but because of the war and the economy, the publication date kept getting put off.

In April 1988, I applied for a passport and my application was approved, but I had no money to travel. On June 3, 1989, Ayatollah Khomeini bid life farewell. Exactly one week later, *Touba and the Meaning of Night* was released. The publisher, worried that it would be confiscated, at first decided to print only 1,500 copies. But during the first six months after its release, the book sold twenty-two thousand copies, and demand remained so high that it was being traded on the black market for many times its cover price. And I was still struggling to pay for my family's basic daily needs.

One night, after having spent hours hand washing our laundry because our washing machine had broken down, I received a phone call. Someone wanted to know whether he should pay the equivalent of two hundred dollars for the book, which normally cost twenty dollars, or wait for the next printing. I was angry. There is nothing more humiliating than poverty. I wrote a letter to a magazine, describing the pressures the government was putting on publishers, the delayed permits, the rationed paper to prevent large print runs, the holding up of deliveries of paper and distribution of finished books. The magazine published my letter and overnight, the editors of a major newspaper pulled their review of *Touba*, which was scheduled to appear the following day, rather than risk angering the government.

But now, publishers were calling and asking me for a new novel. I signed a contract with Esparank for *The Dog and the Long Winter*. I gave *Women Without Men* to Mr. Asslani of Noghreh Publishing again. And I decided to give my next novel to a publishing house called Donyay-e Madar (Mother's World). It was a new house founded by three women and they wanted my new novel to be the first book they published. Still when we met to sign the contract, I warned them that nothing is certain in Iran.

I decided to go to Ramsar, a town on the coast of the Caspian Sea, where I thought I could relax in the vacation home of a friend and begin my next novel. Given that I believed my telephone was tapped and my calls monitored, I decided to call various friends to let them know where I was going and why. I knew this information would be relayed to the authorities in Ramsar through whoever was listening, and I hoped that would allow me to settle in without any trouble.

I arrived at the house in Ramsar and the first thing I saw was a large dead field rat under the mat in front of the door; it was neatly tucked underneath. I called a relative who lived nearby to let her know I had arrived. She warned me that my neighbors to the right were Hezbollah supporters. The following day, I joined my relative to go to the local market. As we walked around the various fruit and vegetable stands, a bearded man walked up to us and asked that we correct our hijab. I looked at myself. I was wearing thick black socks, black shoes, an ankle-length black skirt, a black turtleneck, a black raincoat, and a black headscarf. Other than my face and hands, all that was exposed was about one centimeter of my hairline. My relative, an eighty year old woman, was dressed similarly.

I tried to write. I had no radio and no television, there was nothing interesting to do in town, and I didn't want to go out anyway, since I dreaded having to face more bearded men and their warnings. I was afraid of my neighbors to the right and I could not forget the dead field rat. Nor could I forget the burden of life waiting for me back in Tehran and the agony of my emotional outbursts . . . What was I going to write?

I had to write in a manner that could in no way be interpreted as political or an insult to Islam. That meant avoiding a whole series of subjects. If, in the name of Islam they were killing Muslim children, I had to remain silent. I also had to avoid love and amorous relationships. Love has no meaning in the Islamic Republic. The only acceptable relationship is that of a husband and wife, and even then, I could not write about any interaction between them prior to marriage, unless the man had formally asked for the woman's hand and her family had approved their union. If there was any dialogue between a man and a woman, they had to be either married or siblings. Characters who appear in television or films in the Islamic Republic exist nowhere in the world, not even in Iran. The women are always in full hijab, even in the presence of their husband or children, and there is never any true closeness or sense of intimacy between them.

In *Touba and the Meaning of Night*, I had focused on the pre-revolution era to avoid conflicts with the government. In my new novel, I wanted to look at post-revolution Iran. But whichever way I turned, I faced inevitable self-censorship. In the end, I decided to write about the early years of the revolution in a vague style and then lead the characters back in history, in search of the roots of the issues. I would move the narrative from the real world into a surreal one.

I started to write *Blue Reason*.

Loneliness, my conflicting thoughts and ideas, and the constant feeling that I was being watched were taking a toll on me. Even as a child, I had often felt there was an eye watching me. The feeling was so strong that I would sit with my back to the wall so that the eye could see me only from the front.

I wrote in a passion, and was nearly done in forty days. Then I suddenly went into a trancelike state. For forty-eight hours I didn't eat or sleep. I sat and stared at a fixed spot without making the slightest movement. I was drowned in fantastical thoughts. At some point, a voice started to speak to me. It was loud and clear. Then I started seeing horrifying creatures. Amid all this, a small part of the conscious "me" that had remained alert warned me to try to return to my family.

Traveling in that condition was difficult. I decided to go by the private cars that double as taxis and travel between cities, but I was terrified of the drivers and the other passengers, so I constantly got out of one car and took another. A five-hour drive took twenty-four hours. Along the way, I floated in different worlds, fantasies, nightmares. In Tehran, before making my way back home, I went to different parts of the city. I remember every one of them, but I don't remember how I traveled to these places. I remember riding in a car that had no driver. I remember walking in the rain in the middle of the night. I remember seeing a speck of dust in the palm of my hand and believing that if I stared at it long enough it would multiply and turn into a galaxy. And as I hovered between madness and sanity, the speck of dust did become a galaxy in my mind. All the while, the voice in my head kept telling me that I must keep my feet on the ground, that if I floated in that galaxy, I would be forever cut off from the earth.

Once back home, my family took me to the hospital. There, four people had to hold me down so that the doctor could inject me with a sedative. Twenty-four hours later, I returned home. For two months the voice in my head continued to speak to me. My family didn't understand that I was suffering from a mental illness and didn't know to contact a psychiatrist. The truth is, I was so frightened that I was being followed that I probably would have been too frightened to see a psychiatrist. I didn't trust anyone.

After some time, I began to realize that the voice in my head was telling me things that were not true. I started to control it and tried to test it in different ways to see where its strength came from. Gradually, I learned that the voice knew little about the invisible world, that it had limited knowledge, and that in fact it was my own voice. I started to heal.

In May 1990, *The Dog and the Long Winter* and *Women Without Men* were featured at the national book fair in Tehran. Five thousand copies of *Women Without Men* were sold in one week, and although *The Dog and the Long Winter* had not yet been released, that, too, sold five thousand copies in advance orders. And then the ayatollahs stepped in. Several government sponsored magazines published damning reviews of *Women Without Men*, describing the book as anti-Islam and immoral. Noghreh Publishing's bookstore was raided. When they couldn't find any copies of *Women Without Men*—everything in the bookstore had been sold and there were none left in the warehouse—they went to the publisher of *The Dog and the Long Winter* and confiscated all the remaining copies. A flood of slurs and insults followed. Every day, one of the newspapers published an article attacking me. Other dailies and magazines followed suit. I didn't read any of them, but still, I heard about them from friends.

I had just started earning a little money from the sale of *Touba*. Now, the confiscation of *Women Without Men* and *The Dog and the Long Winter* and the incessant attacks on me and my work meant that not only could I not count on any income from their sales, but *Touba* would not be reprinted. I called Haddad-Adel, the government minister who had helped me when I was first released from prison. He spoke to me in a very dry and dismissive tone, and when I mentioned the attack on *Women Without Men* as immoral, he defended the publisher of one of the most vicious reviews. Thus all that I had managed to achieve was quickly destroyed.

Soon after, I received a letter requesting that I report to the Islamic Revolution Investigations Division. It was all starting again. The only difference was that this time, I was in a fragile and volatile emotional state. I was fed up, tired, and disillusioned.

On the appointed day, I went to the government office. The guards blindfolded me, took me into a room, and sat me down facing the wall. After some time, a man came in and the interrogation started. I remained facing the wall. He asked me why I had discussed virginity in *Women Without Men*. I explained that from a psychological point of view, virginity played a crucial role in the lives of Iranian women, and that the weight of this issue was emotionally crippling them. I went on to explain that women's power of creativity was dissipating into anxiety, stress, and depression, instead of being put to productive use. I added that in the novel, the characters who talk about virginity are two young women aged twenty-eight and thirty-eight, and instead of striving for growth, they live in fear over the question of virginity. I told him that it was important to discuss these topics on a societal level and that doing so could avoid many tragedies.

The interrogator asked, "Why won't you cooperate with the government of the Islamic Republic?" I replied that as a writer I was obliged to remain independent, that I had no particular conflict with the government, and that I would be happy to translate books for their publishing houses. As I spoke, I gradually became more and more irate. I snapped, "Name the most Islamic of these companies and I will go and translate for them."

The session ended. I returned home. Three or four days later, I received a phone call from the Monkerāt Committee, the morality police, summoning me. I asked the man who called to put his request in writing. An hour later, an agent showed up at the house with a letter ordering me to report to their headquarters the following day.

17

THE MONKERĀT COMMITTEE IS A HUGE organization with the power to arrest anyone for anything—wearing thin socks or lipstick, not properly covering your hair, drinking alcohol, being in a car with a member of the opposite sex who is not your immediate kin, being found in possession of music cassettes or video tapes, wearing bright-colored clothes. A rather plump doctor I knew was once arrested because her derriere swayed as she walked. She received several lashes for her crime.

The Monkerāt Committee shares the same public prosecutor's office as the committee that deals with illicit drugs and prostitution, but as it has no prison of its own, most of the people it arrests are held and punished at local detention centers and many are released in exchange for exorbitant indemnity fees.

I went to the Monkerāt Committee headquarters, where I was taken to a room that served as a temporary holding area for women who had been arrested on the city streets. One of my neighbors was there. She said she was at a doctor's office, waiting in the reception area, when the morality police stormed in and arrested everyone, including the doctor and his receptionist. Their offense was nonobservance of proper hijab.

Before I could settle down, my name was called and I was led to an office. There was an investigator and a revolutionary guard there. The guard said, "Look at what you've done to end up at the Monkerāt Committee!"

"I haven't done anything."

"Why did you write about virginity?"

"Because it's an important issue for women. Perhaps you men could write about things that are important to you, such as impotence."

The guard laughed and said, "I know you're an important writer. A few months ago when I was in the presence of Ayatollah Khamenei, he said, 'I read for one half-hour every day and I suggest you all do the same. I recently read a very good book titled *Touba and the Meaning of Night*. You should read it.'"

His comment made me think that perhaps several government factions were in a tug of war and those opposed to Ayatollah Khamenei had decided to arrest me out of spite for him. Of course, I had nothing to do with the ayatollah and, if my theory was correct, why did I have to be the one to pay the price?

The guard said, "You're going to prison."

"Look, sir. Don't try to scare me with prison," I replied. "First of all, I've already spent almost five years in prison with no indictment and no sentence. Second, I'm of the people and there are people in prison, so it doesn't frighten me. Third, I'm under so much pressure and have so many problems that compared to my life, prison sounds like heaven."

I was led to a different room. There, the interrogator wrote a series of routine questions on a sheet of paper. I wrote my answers in such vague prose that no matter how many times the man read them, he couldn't understand what I had written.

They took me back to the women's holding area and then transferred me to the detention center for addicts and drug dealers. For the crime of writing a few sentences about virginity, I was to be locked up alongside drug addicts, smugglers, and prostitutes. Baseless hatred, ignorance, backwardness, conceit, an ancient penchant for sacrificing and being sacrificed, all these had led them to think that by locking me up in this way, they could humiliate me and tarnish my reputation. Later, I learned that someone had called my mother and asked her how long I had been a "user."

I remembered a film I had seen about a priest who was educating a primitive Germanic tribe. The tribesmen would only accept the priest if he let them castrate him without him uttering a sound. And now, I had to suffer incarceration, beatings, and all sorts of cruelty, for them to believe me.

At first I was alone in the room in the detention center. But soon, two other women joined me. One was a wealthy woman who had been arrested because the revolutionary guards had found one half-inch piece of opium in her house. They had also discovered a cassette tape of Hayedeh, a much-loved Iranian singer living in Los Angeles. The other woman had been accused of being a drug addict. She was young, beautiful, tall, and a little plump—the type middle-class men would gladly become slaves to. On our first day, the three of us had to wash some twenty filthy blankets before they would let us sleep at night.

The young woman reminded me of a beautiful girl with

green eyes I had met in Evin Prison. The day she was taken away to be executed, she had told her cellmates, "Girls, believe me, I haven't done anything other than sell a few newspapers. I'm being sacrificed for my green eyes." Every revolutionary guard that came across this girl was tempted to arrest her. And now, this young woman seemed to be suffering from the same destiny. It was clear that she was not addicted to drugs. She didn't even smoke cigarettes.

I liked her. Her behavior toward the guards was very subtle. Although she listened to them and did as they ordered, she ignored their special attentions and managed to keep her distance. Each time one of them made advances toward her, she would raise an eyebrow and with a hint of repugnance in her voice she would say, "Brother, I don't need anyone." One day when I was walking in the courtyard and had my prayer beads in my hand, I heard her say, "My God, she looks just like a priest!" She was right. I was again wearing black from head to toe. I laughed. The young woman had lived a simple life among simple people. I, on the other hand, came from a world where they killed souls.

Five or six days after my arrest, I was taken to a hallway and asked to sit on a bench and wait. There was a room across from where I sat, with three men inside. Two went in and out frequently and sometimes forgot to close the door. The third was handsome and young and sitting behind a desk. In Hezbollah terminology, he had a "luminous aura." In other words, he had fair hair and skin and a certain innocent look reminiscent of Hollywood actors who are often cast in the role of Jesus

Christ. Whenever the door was left open, I could see Luminous Aura. Of course, he never looked at me and was busy working. I watched him for a while and then I wondered if this was all a setup. Perhaps they wanted me to be taken by his good looks so that I could then be accused of immoral behavior. I turned my eyes away from him and started looking around. On the wall in front of me I saw a portrait of the Prophet Ali, which I found strangely fascinating, since Hezbollah was against depicting Islam's holy prophets in religious paintings.

I was getting bored. I had been sitting there for over an hour. I had nothing to do, nothing to read, and I couldn't move from where I was sitting. Finally, with my back against the wall, I sat up very straight and closed my eyes. I didn't want to pretend to be sleeping in a more comfortable position lest they use that as an excuse to harass me. Sitting so rigidly they couldn't possibly find fault with me.

A few minutes later, I was called into the interrogation room. Mr. Asslani, who had published *Women Without Men*, was also there. I felt uneasy. He looked like he, too, had been at the detention center for at least a week.

The cross-examination was vicious. It circled around why I had written the book and why Mr. Asslani had published it. I defended my work and said that I stood firm behind every word I had written. I emphasized that the Ministry of Culture and Islamic Guidance had approved the book and had issued a publishing permit for it. Mr. Asslani also stressed this point and asked the investigator to send someone to his office to fetch the ministry's letter of permission.

The interrogator suddenly flew into a rage. He called some-one and yelled, "Go tell the guys to shut down Noghreh Pub-lishing." Then he ordered several guards to take us back to our detention rooms. I was terribly sorry. Mr. Asslani was a decent man who was trying to live by their rules. He didn't smoke, he never touched alcohol, he didn't even drink coffee or tea. He ran Noghreh together with his wife, an accomplished translator. They were fond of mysticism and most of the books they pub-lished were on that subject. They had also opened a wonderful bookstore where they held monthly art exhibits. Now it was all being confiscated. Before leaving the room, I turned to him and said, "Sir, I truly apologize for having created all these problems for you. I only hope you can forgive me."

After our arrest, a group of writers contacted various gov-ernment departments in the hopes of helping Mr. Asslani and me. But they, too, were under relentless pressure. Two days after the interrogation, I was put on a meat delivery truck and I was transferred to Ghassr Prison. The warden read the warrant for my arrest and sounding surprised, said, "For the crime of writ-ing anti-Islamic works!" And then he asked, "But why have they sent you here?" The unit I was assigned to was designated for addicts, smugglers, and prostitutes. The reason was obvious. If the Monkerāt Committee had turned my file over to the public prosecutor's office, it would no longer have had any say in how my case was handled. But by sending me to the prison for the "morally corrupt," they could keep me under their thumb.

I entered prison for the third time.

Ghassr Prison

18 The prison for drug addicts, narcotics dealers, and prostitutes was worlds apart from the prisons for political detainees. In the prisons I had been to, the political prisoners tried hard to be morally correct and made every effort to read and learn. But the unit in Ghassr Prison where I now found myself was mostly populated with women who had been pushed to the fringes of society from a young age, and they themselves knowingly flaunted this. It was as if it defined them. Most of the prisoners walked in twos, behaving like couples. Many had become exposed to drugs and smuggling while working in brothels, and their only sense of identity was based on sex. Thus, even in prison they had divided themselves into men and women and lived according to a complicated web of rules and customs.

Some of the prisoners were villagers and peasants who had been arrested for smuggling contraband. When I mapped out the regions they came from, I was hardly surprised to see that most were from rural areas along the drug trafficking route that ran through Iran, Afghanistan, and Pakistan. These women were for the most part uneducated and from close-knit families who struggled to make ends meet. I heard many stories along the lines of, "I was standing outside when an Afghan man approached me and asked that I keep a package for him until he returned. And then suddenly the revolutionary guards were there and . . ."

When the women asked me why I had been arrested, I always said because I had written a book. But none of them believed me. Their disbelief was so strong that at times even I doubted whether that was indeed my crime.

A small percentage of the prisoners were educated and even from wealthy families, and for various reasons had fallen victim to addiction. In prison, each of them had a few poor prisoners as servants who washed their clothes and dishes in exchange for a little money. The rural prisoners who were mostly charged with drug-related crimes were penniless and never had any visitors who could bring them money. This was partly because at the time of their arrest many had given the authorities false names. In other cases, the prisoners' relatives had no interest in seeing them, or simply couldn't afford to travel to Tehran.

The food in Ghassr was not only awful, but there was little of it. During the two months I spent there, I never saw a morsel of meat. Once in a while, the cook would add some tofu to the food to compensate for this. Most of the prisoners were always hungry. There was a commissary, but very few could afford to buy anything there. On two or three occasions I bought some canned food and offered some to the women around me. They eagerly accepted without standing on ceremony. But I couldn't go on buying enough food to share with everyone, nor could I sit in front of thirty pairs of hungry eyes and eat better food than they had. I stopped shopping at the commissary.

As time passed I started to grow fond of these women. Our differences faded away and they occasionally confided in me. About eighty-five percent of those charged with trafficking drugs were illiterate. The majority had been married off between the ages of ten and twelve to men who were considerably older than they. Often times, the men had practically bought the girls from peasant families and used them as a partner in bed, a housekeeper, and a vehicle to transport drugs.

One of the drug dealers in the unit was known as Mrs. One Ton. She had been married off to an Afghan drug smuggler when she was only thirteen and eventually started helping him. She was arrested while transporting a hundred kilos of opium. The youngest of her five children was in prison with her. According to some of the women, she had been sentenced to death and was going to be executed.

In political prisons, all the inmates constantly counted prayer beads. We made them from date seeds, which are normally a dull brownish color. We counted them so often that they would become perfectly shiny. But in the prison for prostitutes and addicts, only those women who played the role of the man carried prayer beads. Although the prisoners had accepted that I was independent, I was not sure how they would interpret my counting prayer beads and so I set them aside.

Among the smugglers in the unit was a band of gypsies. In the absence of prayer beads, my pastime became having them tell my fortune. One of them would have been a leader of her community in any other type of society. She was illiterate, but she had an analytical mind and a powerful intelligence. When I told her I was in prison because of a book I had written, she smiled philosophically and said, "Look here, this won't do. What did you really do?" I had no other answer to offer her. She told my fortune using matchsticks. She said she saw an open gate and two men, one short, one tall, waiting for me on the other side. The next day she told my fortune with chickpeas. This time, she said that I would soon find a husband.

One day they brought a young girl to our section. She was small and thin and no more than ten or eleven years old. One of the prisoners who had a daughter of the same age took on the responsibility of caring for the child. I was sitting in the courtyard and the woman came over and asked whether I had anything to eat. For the past forty-eight hours the child and her father and stepmother had been passed around from one government office to another and she had not been given anything to eat. I had a few biscuits and I gave them to her. The woman was overwrought with worry. Seeing the young girl had reminded her of her own children. The young girl's hair was infested with lice and the woman wanted to ask the prison office for some medicated soap so that she could bathe and disinfect the girl.

The next day there was great commotion in the unit. All the prisoners were talking about the young girl. She had told the woman caring for her that her parents were both drug addicts and that her grandfather had regularly raped her. Apparently, the girl had been put in prison because when the police raided their house she had tried to hide her parents' drugs.

I desperately needed to walk and to count my prayer beads. Telling fortunes wasn't going to help at moments like this.

There was a literacy class in prison and I often saw the students come and go. Among them was a woman who was being held in a unit on the second floor. She was always clad is severe hijab and carried a Quran at all times. The prisoners explained that her husband, a revolutionary guard, had accused her of adultery and the court had decided that she should spend five years in prison, after which she would be stoned.

One day I was called to go to the office of the prosecutor in charge of drug-related offenses. I was presented with a letter that stated I would be released in exchange for a hefty bail. I turned down the offer and wrote on the document: "I am innocent, I have committed no offense, and I have no money to post bail."

They took me back to my unit. Out in the courtyard, I saw Mrs. One Ton and her young son and another woman with her infant daughter. The baby was blond and blue eyed, very beautiful and very quiet. Having fed on her drug-addicted mother's milk, the infant, too, was addicted. A few hours later, the baby started to fuss. She needed to be changed. But her mother callously kicked her aside.

It was one of those rare moments in life when I wanted to beat someone mercilessly. I was incensed. I turned to Mrs. One Ton and said, "You see? Now do you understand why they execute drug smugglers? Look at that child!" Mrs. One Ton clutched her son in her arms. The infant girl lay on the ground, quietly looking around. Another prisoner hurried over and picked her up and changed her diaper. The child's mother, terrified of being punished, quickly got busy tending to her daughter.

I remembered Mother Mossana who had offered her boys with both hands to the turbulent political currents in the country, and then there were the miserable women in this prison who were drowning in a swamp of corruption and misery and dragging their children down with them.

A week after I turned down the offer of freedom in exchange for a large sum of money, I was again summoned to the prison administration office. After two months in Ghassr Prison, I was being released. I was led to the front gate and set free. It was against the law. I should have been taken to the Monkerāt Committee headquarters for my release to be processed.

Once again, my family was waiting for me outside the prison gates. My mother had asked my aunt to put up her house as collateral and she had signed my bail document. This, too, was against the law. Only I could sign my bail agreement. Later, my mother explained that she had also sent a letter to Ayatollah Khamenei pleading my innocence.

Tehran

19 I WAS OUT OF PRISON, BUT I HAD NO money and no way to support myself. The Monkerāt Committee had the manuscript of my new novel, *Blue Reason*, and publication had been delayed. I gave some friends photocopies of the manuscript for safekeeping and hoped desperately to find a way to send one copy overseas. Meanwhile, Noghreh Publishing was no longer allowed to publish my works.

I kept thinking about the letter my mother had written to Ayatollah Khamenei. Several people were urging me to write to him myself. If I didn't, it would seem as if I had asked my mother to plead on my behalf. I sat and wrote the letter. After explaining that I was a writer and that I had been sent to prison several times without having been formally charged with a crime, I wrote that a revolutionary guard at the Monkerāt Committee had told me that the ayatollah had once encouraged them to read my book. I went on to describe the prisons, I wrote about the girls who had been married off when they were still children, and I wrote about their poverty and illiteracy. I also wrote about Noghreh Publishing and the injustice that was done to its owners, and I wrote that now my new novel, *Blue Reason*, had been seized.

I made three copies of the letter and mailed each under a different sender's name, just in case a letter with my name might be confiscated. At the post office, the clerk looked at the envelopes and said with disgust, "You write to these people?" I don't know if my letters ever reached their destination.

We put the home we had inherited from my father up for sale to raise money and I signed a contract to translate a one-thousand-page Chinese novel. I spent my days translating and guiding potential buyers through the house. In that suffocating atmosphere, I paced the rooms and dreamed of money. I had given up thinking about humanity, its future, the role of the writer, the creation of a better society. All I thought about was money; enough money to create a comfortable life for my family and to build a fence around us to keep out trouble and misfortune. The key to doing all this was money. Money, money, money.

Monarchists, democrats, nationalists, liberals, socialists, communists, the Mujahedin, the Kurds, and religious minorities had all fled overseas. Two-thirds of the country's prominent writers were now scattered throughout the world. Amid all this, what need was there for me to write? If I wanted to prove I was a writer, I had already done so. Did I have anything new to say? Of course I did. My mind was ready to blossom with new ideas. But instead of sitting and deliberating with like-minded peers, organizing lectures, and exchanging ideas with people, I had been locked up in a prison for drug addicts and prostitutes.

I was lonely. I regretted that I had not pursued a financially rewarding career. If I had become a doctor, or an architect, or even if I had opened a convenience store, I wouldn't have to worry about the future and I wouldn't shudder at the thought of being penniless. From that time on, there has not been a single moment when I have not thought about money.

In February 1991, two films by Mohsen Makhmalbaf were selected to be screened at the Fajr Festival, the annual film festival in Tehran. I had met Makhmalbaf at the home of my ex-husband, and would have liked to see the films, but I knew my going to the festival would create an uproar. Following the festival, both films came under attack by the government and were banned from further screenings. What struck me as strange was that from that point on, all media censures directed at Makhmalbaf also criticized me. It was as if we were a team and our names were linked. This went on for quite a while, but I never understood the reason why.

In late winter 1992, we sold our house. On our first day in our new home, I was busy moving boxes when the telephone rang. I was surprised; we hadn't given our new telephone number to anyone yet. It was someone from the Monkerāt Committee. He informed me that I was under surveillance and that I should appear in court the following week.

On the day of my hearing, the two officers from the Ministry of Culture and Islamic Guidance who had issued a publishing permit for *Women Without Men* were not present, nor was Mr. Asslani, who was ill. The prosecutor asked me why I had written the novel. I defended my book and said that I found nothing wrong with its content. The court clerk had found the word "prostitute" in *The Dog and the Long Winter*. He turned to me and asked, "Why did you commit such impertinence?" I explained that sometimes a writer has to write dialogue in the same language and tone as is spoken by the general public. I added that in Persian the word *jendeh* (whore) originally meant "lady," that it was still used with that definition among the Persian-speaking population of Afghanistan, and that it was not my fault if every word related to women was eventually transformed to mean something ugly and unseemly, including the word "madam."

The court made no decision and my case was postponed. They still retained the deed to my aunt's house as bail and I could see that this would be used as a weapon against me.

About two years earlier, I had received an invitation from the House of World Cultures in Berlin to give a lecture. I had my passport now, so I wrote to them asking whether their invitation was still open. News of what I had experienced had spread overseas, and they quickly wrote back, asking me to visit. Then I received an invitation from the Iranian Women's Studies Foundation in the US to appear at one of their events in the spring of 1993. Soon other invitations to attend literary events followed.

I decided to go to Germany and from there to Sweden and then to the US. But first, I had to find a way to close my case file at the Monkerāt Committee and release my aunt's house.

In December 1992, I went to the Committee to discuss my case, but I was told that my file had been transferred to the public prosecutor's office and that it no longer concerned them.

I went to the public prosecutor's office and was told that a hearing was scheduled for early March. I bought an airplane ticket for April. But if the two officers from the Ministry of Culture and Islamic Guidance did not appear in court, my case would again be postponed. I contacted the publishers of my books and asked them to speak to the officers and try to convince them to attend the hearing. Their efforts only resulted in their being accused of interfering in ministerial affairs.

On the day of the hearing, the officers did not show up. The case was again postponed. In twenty days I was to board a flight to Germany. I didn't know what to do. I went to visit my aunt and told her about my plans. She was worried and she had every right to be.

I returned home and sat down to take measure of my life. I had been in prison three times, but because I had always been poor, I had managed to stay free in a different respect. Poverty is devastating, but its benefit is that you have nothing to lose. And I had always lived in such a way that I would never be in anyone's debt. Now I was indebted to my aunt and had completely lost my freedom.

On the morning of March 13, 1993, I packed some toiletries, a few pieces of clothing, and some money and went to the prosecutor's office together with my brother. I had decided to turn myself in and release the house. The official I met with was overjoyed. He got up and walked out of his office and quickly returned with the warrant for my arrest. My brother and I were amazed at the speed with which he processed the paperwork. In truth, I had thought that the man would try to dissuade me from what I was about to do and would even suggest a legal channel through which I could bring my case to a close.

I asked permission to call my aunt and have her meet us there. She arrived and I waited while the process of releasing the deed was completed. Then the official called an officer and handed me over to him. I was put on a minibus with other detainees and we were taken to Evin Prison, which by then had been transformed from a political prison to a regular one. The warden in charge of the temporary detention area was polite and seemed sorry to see me there. He walked me down various hallways and at the entrance to a unit turned me over to the women guards. I entered prison for the fourth time.

Evin Prison, December 1992

20 THE TEMPORARY DETENTION AREA at Evin Prison, where all prisoners in transit spent their first and last few days, was the filthiest place I had ever seen in my life. It was a large room with a squat toilet stall in a corner. The toilet was often clogged and overflowing, and the prisoners would walk in the spillover and with the same shoes step on the blankets where we sat, ate, and slept. The blankets had not been washed in years; there was nowhere for us to wash them. More blankets were piled up alongside the walls. These were our cover at night and were equally foul.

This time, I found myself among a crowd of thieves, pickpockets, prostitutes, and murderers. I saw the girl I had met two years earlier at Ghassr Prison who had been repeatedly raped by her grandfather. She had just returned from court and was in the company of a few older women who seemed to be madams. It looked as if they were prepping her for the future. There was a group of young women in another corner. One kept insisting that she was a virgin and should not be locked up.

Before long, the door opened and another prisoner was ushered in. She was about fifty years old. She said she had been arrested for fraud but she had not meant to swindle her victim, she had definitely intended to pay the lady for her jewelry. Her proof of innocence was her virginity, which she constantly talked about. She spent most of her time reading the Quran, until she decided to unclog the toilet and stuck the water hose we used to wash ourselves in the toilet bowl. Now we had the dilemma of how to clean ourselves after using the toilet.

The following night, the room was empty. Most of the women had either been released or transferred to a permanent unit. The young girl I had met previously was still there, so were the women who had been keeping her company. It was raining hard and suddenly there was a deafening peal of thunder. Terrified, the girl jumped up, ran to the middle of the room, wrapped her arms around herself, and burst into tears. I am not a gentle person, but I automatically went over and took her in my arms. She tried to break free, but I held her tight and did not let her go. She finally calmed down and I let her go back to where she was sitting. I followed her and sat down next to her. Then I quietly said, "Lightning is nothing to be afraid of. It's the same light that you see in this light bulb. Are you frightened of the light bulb?" I went on to explain why thunder and lightning strike during a storm. She listened intently, so did the other women. They were all illiterate. I thought how easy it was to create myths for these women, to mold them into beings capable of doing almost anything, perhaps even murder.

I was transferred to a regular prison unit that was populated primarily by women who had been arrested following a government initiative to eradicate prostitution. The revolutionary guards had raided the neighborhood that had served as Tehran's red light district prior to the revolution, although under the Islamic Republic, such neighborhoods supposedly no longer existed. The guards had burned down the buildings, destroyed the women's belongings, and herded them into prison. Given that each prostitute had to pay a large fine, arresting them was a lucrative business. The extorted fee had replaced the tax that was imposed on brothels during the shah's regime.

The girls arrested during the raid had all been badly beaten. Without exaggeration, they were all missing teeth. Each one who shared her story would immediately open her mouth to prove what had been done to her. I had come across many addicts, smugglers, and prostitutes in prison, but none had been so violently tortured as these women. And they had all been sentenced to very long prison terms.

I was transferred again, this time to a unit where the majority of inmates were political prisoners. Among the nonpolitical prisoners, there were many women who had murdered their husbands. Later, I learned from an official in the public prosecutor's office that prior to the revolution it was mostly men who ended up in prison for killing their wives, but the statistics changed after the revolution. Of course, the men were right to no longer kill their wives; the government was taking care of this for them.

It was in this unit that I learned the woman I had met in Ghassr Prison who had been accused of adultery by her husband, and who was sentenced to spend five years in prison before being stoned, had miraculously escaped her fate. She was taken to the site of her stoning and buried up to her neck in the ground. But just as people started throwing stones, the earth around her suddenly caved in, freeing her body. This was interpreted as a miracle proving the woman's innocence. She was given a pardon and sent home. Perhaps to her husband's home.

A series of holidays came one after the other—the anniversary of the founding of the Islamic Republic, Ramadan, and the new year. Meanwhile, the Mujahedin launched a series of attacks against several Islamic Republic embassies in Europe. What it all meant was that my case was no longer on anyone's mind.

21

THEY INSTALLED TELEPHONES IN prison. Inmates could now call outside. Doubtless, it was the result of efforts by international organizations. It was during a telephone conversation with my family that I learned a friend had vouched for me and offered guarantees in exchange for my release.

On the day I was being discharged, a guard at the unit door decided to inspect my bag. I had seen many prisoners leave without an inspection. Oftentimes, there wouldn't even be a guard at the door. I assumed she was just curious and wanted to see if I had bought any handcrafts made by the prisoners. She emptied my bag and carefully examined two sequined belts that I had bought from one of the women. She asked how much I had paid for them. I thought if I told her the truth, she would probably extort money from the girl who had made them. I gave her a false price. Then she caught sight of my notebook. She took it and said, "This has to stay here until officials decide what to do with it."

I said, "But I need the notebook and must take it with me."

"You can't."

"Why not?"

"The prisoners may have written letters in it for you to deliver."

"There are telephones in prison and the prisoners can contact whoever they want. They don't need to write letters."

I grabbed the notebook, tore it into four pieces, threw it down on the table, and snapped, "Here's the notebook. Please take it."

The guard quickly called the warden and I was returned to the unit. A short while later, I was led to the prison administration office where three men were waiting for me. One of them was a strong-looking young man who was sitting behind a desk. He asked, "Why did you tear up the notebook?" I replied, "I had written some private things in it. If I had ripped it up in the unit, you would never have known I had it. So, instead, I tore it up as I was leaving."

He shouted, "Shut up!" And he picked up the teacup sitting on his desk and hurled it at me. It hit me in the face. Then he leaped up from his chair, rushed toward me, and punched me several times on the left side of my face. "Get over there and stand facing the wall!" he yelled. I did as he ordered. It was strange. I didn't feel insulted at all. I realized that I had considered these people small and petty for so long, that now they were truly insignificant to me, even when they beat me.

The man barked, "Now I'm going to ask you again and I want a proper answer. Why did you tear up the notebook?"

"I had written some private things in it. If I had ripped it up in the unit, you would never have known I had it. So, instead, I tore it up as I was leaving."

"Private matters. I see!"

It became obvious that, as with all the interrogators and investigators I had come across over the years, he, too, was hoping to find a promiscuous subtext to my actions. He started flipping through the torn pieces of paper and came across a phrase—something like "streams of rain and glittering light." He read it out loud to his friends so that they could help him discover its underlying indecency.

Eventually, I was led out into the hallway where I spent the night sitting on a bench. My family, believing I was being released, had come to prison and I was allowed to briefly meet with them. They were extremely worried; they had just been told that I would be executed. "In that case," I said, "I will say goodbye to you." But instead of being executed, I was returned to the temporary detention room.

The following morning, I was put on a minibus and driven out of the prison compound. I thought I was being released, but the driver took me to the public prosecutor's office. The official in charge of the department that dealt with my case was shocked when he saw my bruised face. He exclaimed, "Ma'am, why do you do these things? We went through a lot of trouble to have you released." I wanted to say, I'm sorry, your prehistoric traditions got the better of me. But I decided not to joke. He explained that the prison guard who had inspected my bag claimed that I tried to strangle her and that she had struggled to save herself. The torn pieces of my notebook, proof of the guard's claims, were sitting on his desk. I said, "I, too, have a grievance. I was beaten for no reason and I request that I be taken to the medical examiner to be checked." He asked me to write down what had happened.

I wrote a detailed account of the previous day and handed it to him. He read it carefully, jotted down a few words, and handed the papers to the minibus driver who was waiting at the door. Then he said goodbye to me and left. He said nothing about sending me to the medical examiner and I decided that if I were released I would go there myself. The driver glanced at the papers and exclaimed, "This is impossible! It's a warrant for your arrest!" Justice was hard at work to break the last stupid Iranian who believed one should fight for democracy.

I was returned to the temporary detention room at Evin Prison. The next day I was blindfolded and taken to a different building. They only blindfolded political prisoners. It was a stupid game. I was led into a room and my blindfold was removed. I sat there for a while until a man walked in and said that he was from the prosecutor's office and that he was hoping to bring my case to a close. He explained that the complaint filed by the prison guard was serious and that it could put my life in danger. But, he added, if I agreed to cooperate with them, all would end well. He was relatively polite, so I told him that my only crime was that people liked my work, that my books had sold well, and therefore certain groups were trying to either break me or coerce me into cooperating with them.

Suddenly, my tears began to flow and again, I started to scream. Once more, I was asked to write down my side of the story. Just as I was about to start, the man stopped me and said it was better if the document was in his handwriting. He wrote a page and read it back to me. It was relatively accurate, but he had left out my grievance against the man who had beaten me. Regardless, the only thing I objected to was his use of the word *bandeh*—meaning slave or servant—each time I made reference to myself. I asked him to change it to "I." He looked surprised and said, "We are all servants of God." I replied, "That is true. I am a servant of God. But I'm not writing this note to God."

In my view, in traditional Iranian culture, the notion of "I" is eradicated. As individuals, each person is considered to be a *bandeh*. But to me, a slave needs an owner; she cannot think for himself, she cannot create anything, and she doesn't have an independent thought.

I was released the next day. My eye was still bruised. I returned home and started preparing to leave the country. Although I had missed my lecture in Germany, I still had time to make it to the event in the US. But first I had to travel to Switzerland to apply for a US visa.

My son's birthday was two days away and he had invited a few of his friends over to celebrate. Together we went to do some shopping for the party. As I was driving down a highway near my home, a military police SUV suddenly swerved into my car. For an instant, I thought it was an assassination attempt. But the SUV was spinning out of control, too. Miraculously, we did not crash into other cars on the highway. The SUV came to a stop at the edge of the highway and my car rolled over and landed on its right side. I was thrown into the backseat and landed on my head. My son managed to climb out the window on the driver's side and came to help me crawl through the shattered rear window. I had barely made it out when one of the two military police officers, who had climbed out of the wrecked SUV, shouted, "Sister, fix your hijab!" The broken glass had cut my right ear and disarranged my headscarf. I didn't realize my ear had been cut until hours later when I returned home and took off my headscarf.

One of my neighbors was among the people who had gathered around the accident site. He had been driving some distance behind me and the SUV had passed him at a speed of at least ninety miles per hour. He said he had turned to the other man in his car and said, God save the cars up ahead . . . Just then he had seen the SUV swerve into my car and spin out of control.

A few minutes later, the traffic police arrived, as did my brother, who had been called by another neighbor who had witnessed the accident. It turned out that the young officer driving the SUV did not have a driver's license. The policeman drew an outline of the accident site and determined that I was at fault. Astonished, my brother and I politely disagreed with him and pointed to black brake marks on the asphalt where the SUV had suddenly swerved to the right. It was useless.

We went to the police station, where all my explanations were equally futile. Finally, fed up and frustrated, I screamed at the police officer, "I wish with all my heart that you drop dead and that your mother never stops mourning!" The end result was that the officer not only took my driver's license and insurance papers, but he demanded that we produce a deed to a property as security for my release.

I thought of my struggle to rid myself of the burden of the deed to my aunt's house that had been used as collateral for my release from Evin. But all our efforts to dissuade the officer were ignored. Finally, my brother left and returned sometime later with the deed to another relative's house.

I spent the next several days desperately trying to close the cases against me. After finally completing my case file with the Monkerāt Committee, I had to go to the records office to finalize the paperwork. There, several people were quietly breaking the seals on various files, adding or taking out documents, and resealing them.

To follow up on my car accident, I had to go to the military police headquarters where I met with a senior officer who, after a lot of theatrics, let me know that they accepted no liability and would not cover the damages to my car.

I thanked God for having blessed me with these scenes before I left Iran. In those years, people were so frustrated with the government that in the absence of any kind of political opposition all they could do was yearn for the pre-revolution days. Taxi drivers, newspaper sellers, shopkeepers, people standing on line for meat and cheese and bread, all were hailing the shah and feeling nostalgic for the old days. I, too, thought the old days better. Even though we suffered the tyranny of the SAVAK, lived with widespread corruption, and I'd been imprisoned then also, I at least used to have the freedom to dress the way I wanted to.

In any case, my car was old and had seen better days and I had no money to have it repaired. I put it up for sale and a few days before I left Iran I sold it to an eager young man. And I thought, long live the West, at least there they can produce a car that still has some value, even as a cadaver.

22

I WAS ON BOARD A SWISSAIR FLIGHT to Los Angeles. I spent the first few hours writing the speech I wanted to give at the conference organized by the Iranian Women's Studies Foundation. After many months, this was the first opportunity I had to calmly collect my thoughts. In prison, I had spent many hours thinking about what I wanted to say, but this was the first time I could do so without fear. All doors were open to me. I could talk about anything I wanted and for as long as I wanted.

I knew if I spoke openly about what I had witnessed and experienced, I would not be able to return to Iran. I decided that it didn't matter. Like thousands of others, I could find a place to live somewhere else in the world. Still, I had to tread carefully. My family was in Iran and my actions could put them in danger.

I had no intention of saying anything that could be construed as an attack against Islam. Islam is the faith of ninety-nine percent of the people of Iran, sixty percent of whom live in far-flung rural areas with meager means and without the least comfort. They live relying on their faith. What's more, Islam was not the cause of the ills in Iran. It was the fundamentalist interpretation of the faith that had brought about the tragedy that continued to unfold.

Meanwhile, I made a decision on how best to deal with the issue of hijab. At each event, I would walk up to the podium with a headscarf draped on my shoulders. I would explain that I was against mandatory hijab. Then, I would take the headscarf and cover my hair. At the end of my talk, I would take it off and leave the podium. This way, I hoped my audiences would know that I objected to hijab, but seeing me wear it, they would realize I was not free to speak openly. Some people understood this; many others did not and objected to my hijab.

My visit to the US brought me the gift of many dear friends. From there, I was invited to Canada. At an event in Ottawa, I again started my talk by going through the ceremony with my headscarf. During the question and answer period that followed, a well-dressed, bearded man walked up to me and rudely tossed a piece of paper in front of me. He had written, "Do you think it is right for you to disgrace hijab in this manner?" I assumed he was attached to the Islamic Republic's embassy in Ottawa.

There were two girls sitting in the back of the room wearing colorful floral headscarves. Later, at the reception, they came up to me. One of them looked very familiar. I thought she was perhaps one of the political prisoners I had met in prison. When I asked her, "Have you ever been to prison?" She said, "Yes . . . no . . ." That night, I was jolted from my sleep. I suddenly remembered the girl. She was a guard at Evin Prison who one day had for no reason showered me with vulgar insults. Obviously, she had been promoted.

I traveled to Sweden next; I was starting to feel tired and worn-out. I was in Stockholm when I learned that a bomb had exploded in front of Noghreh Publishing's offices in Tehran. I called and spoke to a few staff members. There was no doubt in my mind that there was a connection between the bearded man, the two girls, and the bomb.

I was devastated and emotionally unwell. I didn't know who would benefit if I were to speak up and speak openly. With the exception of the Mujahedin, all political opposition groups had for all practical purposes disintegrated. I didn't know how to compensate the losses Noghreh Publishing had suffered. All they had done was publish a book. Ever since *Women Without Men* had been confiscated, it was being photocopied and secretly sold in the black market by the thousands for a hefty price. I assumed that the people selling the photocopies were connected to the Hezbollah—no one else would dare try to make a profit from it. And now the publisher had suffered an even greater loss.

I was in Sweden for thirteen days, during which I had to travel to ten cities. I robotically went from town to town and then left for Germany, where I was also to speak at ten events in ten cities during a two-week stay. After that, a two-city stop in Norway, then Vienna, and finally the UK. I was in London when I was struck by the same symptoms I had experienced while writing *Blue Reason* at my friend's vacation house in Ramsar. I was not only crippled by the fear that there were hidden cameras in my hotel room, but I also believed that my mind could be remotely manipulated and thoughts and images could be inserted in my brain.

I did not sleep for several days, and my agitation grew worse. Luckily, I had a relative in London, who came to take me to her home. On the way there, I saw a young boy on the subway who looked like Ahmad-Reza, the boy at Ghezel-Hessar Prison who reminded me of the *Little Prince*. In my fevered mind, I believed that a man in the Islamic Republic government had raped the boy so that the blessing of the boy's existence would be transferred to him. After the rape, the boy had gone mad. The torment of this delusion was so enormous that I could barely remain still on the train. Soon the horror spread to include all the young children I knew. Then I imagined that all the brave men I knew, grief-stricken over the rape of the children, had castrated themselves and gone to battle with the Islamic Republic's demons.

Although this madness was my own, I wonder if societies can be struck by a similar sort of collective insanity. When pressure mounts beyond the people's tolerance, do they abandon all beliefs and begin to exist in an illusory world of their own creation? In that state, will they believe everything they are told?

My relative took me to a hospital. By then, I had become obsessed with images I had seen of three American astronauts in a space shuttle, taking photographs of the earth. Now, the astronauts seemed to be dead, but because of certain elements in outer space, they were continuing a different kind of existence. In the photographs they had taken, they had seen all the people who had been executed in Iran. They were transferring the corpses into space and the dead were coming back to life. I knew that reconstructing those lost Iranians would take time, and I believed that because the astronauts had gone mad and died above the earth's atmosphere, they had determined that I should drape a towel over my shoulder, put my duffle bag on top of it, and remain standing all night. And so I stood in my hospital room in that comical position from dusk until dawn. I was near collapse from exhaustion, but I knew that if I slept the dead would not come back to life. Golshan was among them. She was coming to life, but she still couldn't remember herself.

Perhaps there is some logic to the illogical actions of the insane. If one can bring hundreds of executed youth back to life by standing up all night, then one should stand up all night. And if it means that a crazy astronaut will demand that you cover your shoulder with a towel and hold your duffle bag over it, so be it.

I was in the hospital for more than a month. I had been admitted as an emergency patient and was not required to pay for my hospitalization and treatment. Otherwise, even if I were to pawn my entire life, I would not have been able to cover the costs. The doctors and the hospital staff were the personification of humanity. As a writer in my own country, I had been subjected to harassment and injustice. But as a stranger in a hospital in London, I was extended every kindness and respect. I will always be grateful.

When I was released from the hospital, I flew to Switzerland, planning to take a connecting flight to Iran. En route, I tore up all my papers and notes. At the airport in Switzerland, I put on my headscarf and went to check in for my Iran Air flight. They refused to accept my suitcase unless I paid for the extra weight. I had traveled to exactly forty-two cities with the exact same suitcase and no airline had made such a demand. I paid the fee.

There was a man with a thick bushy beard and the bearing of a hangman standing at the entrance to the plane. The flight attendant checking the passengers' tickets was in full hijab. Deep inside, I felt as if my back was bent, and I was being asked to grovel. At Tehran's Mehrabad Airport, the passengers waited exactly four hours for their luggage. I thought of the one year I had spent traveling to forty-two cities without ever having to wait more than a half hour to receive my bag. Finally, the suitcases arrived. Mine was completely banged up and there was a muddy footprint on it.

Departure

23 I SPENT THE NEXT YEAR MOSTLY SIT-
ting and staring at the wall. I couldn't write.
On the one hand, the strong medications I
was taking stifled my imagination, and on the
other, I didn't know what to write about. I had
lost hope for the future of Iranian society. I had seen the progress and technological advancements on the other side of the
world and, in comparison, I felt that my side of the world was
moving backward to a distant past. The strange stubbornness of
the traditional forces in the country had brought progress to a
halt. Perhaps the Islamic Republic's leaders think that by bringing the country to a cultural standstill they will guarantee their
own longevity.

I went on several trips with my friends. In Mashad, once
a major oasis along the ancient Silk Road, the moment we set
foot in the city bazaar, two women approached me and asked
that I fix my hijab. I was wearing an ugly, ill-fitting coverall
that went down to my ankles. My headscarf was pulled forward and all that was revealed was my hairline. I said, "Madam,
they will not be burying me in your grave. Jesus minds his own
faith, Moses minds his own . . ." The woman quickly called a

"brother"—a bearded man with a frightening face. They threatened to take me to the committee. My friends quickly launched into theatrics, brought the matter to a close, and led me away.

We traveled to Kashan. I suggested we forgo visiting the bazaar and instead visit the public gardens. As we were leaving, two "sisters" suggested I correct my hijab and again, a "brother" was called to deal with me. We went to Isfahan, which was once a major international tourist attraction. Now the city was suffocating under a blanket of smog and pollution. At Chehel Sotoun Pavilion, a magnificent structure originally built by Shah Abbas II in the seventeenth century, two massive portraits of Ayatollah Khamenei and Ayatollah Rafsanjani were hanging from two sides of the pavilion, completely ruining the building's beautiful façade. The majority of the tourists were all clad in black from head to toe. It seemed as if they were there for a funeral.

Back in Tehran, a friend suggested we go hiking once a week. In the absence of sporting and entertainment facilities, Iranian youth had taken to the mountains and the trails were always packed with people. At the foot of the mountain, where buses dropped off hikers, there were always two sisters and a brother checking everyone. It was all about luck. They stopped a young man and argued with him over the top button on his shirt, which was open, while ten other young men walked by with their shirt collars similarly unbuttoned. One day, a guard arrested a young couple because he claimed he had seen them through his binoculars holding hands while walking up a trail.

After a year of this, I had had enough. When I received an invitation to participate in an event in Germany, I did not hesitate. I had to live elsewhere for a while, just so that I could breathe.

I have never returned to Iran.

Acknowledgments

BELIEVE EVERYTHING HAS A SPIRIT, EVEN SEEM-
ingly lifeless objects. I believe spirits are active and at times,
for reasons that remain unknown to me, their actions become
palpable.

I believe the girls who were led to the execution grounds
sent their spirits back to sit on my shoulders. For years, I have
carried their weight. By writing this memoir, I am trying to
unburden myself. In truth, there is little else I can do.

In the course of the eight-year Iran-Iraq war, one million
young men lost their lives. They walked across mine fields,
threw themselves in front of tanks, sacrificed themselves in so
many other ways, and for years their bodies remained in the
wastelands. Again, there is little that I can do to show gratitude
for their sacrifice.

I wrote this book in the hopes of honoring the executed
victims of the Islamic Republic. I will take this opportunity to
dedicate the spirit of this book to the martyrs of that futile war
and the victims of the government.

There are many dear friends to whom I owe great thanks.
I always hoped that someday I would be wealthy enough to
express my gratitude by offering them valuable gifts. Unfortu-

nately, this is not likely to happen. Therefore, I will name them here.

Nima Mina, who has translated my work, Masoud Mafan, my publisher in Sweden, Sara Khalili, who translated this edition of my prison memoir, Gloria Jacobs, my editor and publisher at the Feminist Press, and Robert Coover and Shirin Neshat, who have each been a great friend and supporter of my work.

I had many friends and supporters during my travels. They include Isabel Allende, Amy Tan, Alice Parker, Jon Carol, Eskandar Abadi, Shahin Asayesh, Mahnaz Afkhami, Minu Afshar, Soheila Amin, Goli Amin, Dr. Nasser Pakdaman, Gelayol Panbehchi, Ali Jadidi, Dr. Mohammad-Ali Jazayeri, Siamak Jahanbakhsh, Dr. Dadsetan, Pari Dastmalchi, Hayedeh Daragahi, Mohammad Rahimian, Majid Roshangar, Martin Gilet, Shahla and Ali Siami, Hassan Sattarian, Dr. and Mrs. Manouchehr Shayegan, Dr. Azita Shafazand, Favad Saberan, Shahran Tabari, Mr. and Mrs. Agheli, Ali Erfan, Professor Bozorg Alavi, Sussan Amid, Bayesteh Ghaffari, Elham Gheytanchi, Mohammad Reza Ghanoonparvar, Simin Karimi, John Guerney, Habib Lajevardi, Gilbert Lazare, Shohreh Maleki, Nassrin Motahedeh, Cyrus Moshki, Hamid Mohamedi, Steve McDowell, Mehrnoush Mazareii, Marjan Mohtashemi, the Mashouf family, Mizban, Farzaneh Milani, Homa Nategh, Afsaneh Najmabadi, Jamileh Nedaii, Michael Hillman, and Farzin Yazdanfar. Kamran Talatoff and Hava Houshmand, who translated my book *Touba and the Meaning of Night* into English, and . . . I have forgotten tens of other names. I take this opportunity to thank all who were my hosts. I worry there may not be another opportunity for me to recognize their kindness to me. The people I have named live in different countries and many of them don't know each other. Their faiths and beliefs are different. What they have in common is being Iranian or an Iranologist, and the fact that they supported me because "someone has written books, let us show appreciation."

I truly hope that by extending my thanks to these people I will not have created difficulties for them.

The Feminist Press is an independent, nonprofit literary publisher that promotes freedom of expression and social justice. Founded in 1970, we began as a crucial publishing component of second wave feminism, reprinting feminist classics by writers such as Zora Neale Hurston and Charlotte Perkins Gilman, and providing much-needed texts for the developing field of women's studies with books by Barbara Ehrenreich and Grace Paley. We publish feminist literature from around the world, by best-selling authors such as Shahrnush Parsipur, Ruth Kluger, and Ama Ata Aidoo; and North American writers of diverse race and class experience, such as Paule Marshall and Rahna Reiko Rizzuto. We have become the vanguard for books on contemporary feminist issues of equality and gender identity, with authors as various as Anita Hill, Justin Vivian Bond, and Ann Jones. We seek out innovative, often surprising books that tell a different story.

See our complete list of books at **feministpress.org**, and join the Friends of FP to receive all our books at a great discount.

THE FEMINIST PRESS
AT THE CITY UNIVERSITY OF NEW YORK
FEMINISTPRESS.ORG